SERVICE, SACRIFICE, LOYALTY

★

GUARDING FREEDOM'S FLAME

BY CONNIE CLARK

TABLE OF CONTENTS

FOREWORD

FOREWORD

The heritage of freedom is etched into the souls of America's people. Over and over again, American soldiers have responded to the call and shed their blood on the battlefields at Yorktown, Antietam, Cuba, the Philippines, at the Second Battle of the Marne in France, and on the shores of Normandy. Korea's Inchon Peninsula and Vietnam's Mekong Delta claimed more of our sons and daughters. Lebanon, Quemoy, Grenada, and Panama also extracted a high human price for freedom.

The stirring words of President John F. Kennedy's inaugural address epitomize the premium of freedom we as a nation are willing to pay dearly for:

"In the long history of the world, only a few generations have been granted the role of defending freedom in its hour of maximum danger. I do not shrink from this responsibility; I welcome it. I do not believe that any of us would exchange places with any other people or any other generation. The energy, the faith, the devotion which we bring to this endeavor will light our country and all who serve it, and the glow from that fire can truly light the world."

Our veterans bore the brunt of defending our liberty, and they executed their duties with courage, steadfastness, and good spirits. We try to remember them on certain days of the year, holidays such as Veterans Day and Memorial Day, but I'm afraid many don't bear in mind the supreme sacrifices we asked them to make—sacrifices they made without a moment's hesitation.

Our great nation has a proud history of soldiering. More than 216 years ago, America's first patriots pledged their lives to the ideal of freedom. Both with their ink and their blood, these men founded the American nation on the principles of individual rights and the spirit of liberty. Of the forty men who signed the Constitution of the United States, twenty-three fought in the War for Independence. They were America's first defenders of freedom.

These brave, inspired men created a tradition of citizensoldiers—farmers, merchants, and craftsmen in peacetime, fighting patriots in battle. Each stepped forward eagerly to answer America's call to independence, and they made it possible for us to enjoy the fruits of our land and the liberties they so painstakingly designed.

They did not seek war, but they understood the necessity of battle when our borders or our freedoms were threatened. Many gave their lives in defense of a single, shining principle: freedom.

Men and women of our country have continued to answer the call whenever peace and freedom were jeopardized. Our cherished values can only be preserved when citizens are willing to defend it. That is our distinct American heritage.

The "Boys of '98" helped put America on the world map when they signed up to fight a two-pronged war, one in the nearby Caribbean islands of Cuba and Puerto Rico, the other in the remote Philippines. The Spanish-American War and the insurrection in the Philippines proved more challenging than anticipated. Although only 362 servicemen died in combat on Cuba, some 2,621 died from non-hostile causes, mostly diseases such as dysentery and typhoid fever. Medical treatment was poor or unavailable; the food was often inedible; camps were filthy, damp, and intemperate; and clothing for the troops was inadequate.

Tropical disease swept through the military camps in Cuba, placing more than 4,000 men on the sick list in the Fifth Army Corps. As many as 20,000 veterans of Cuba were sent back to the States, and many were quarantined. Some were described by a historian of the war as arriving home with a "death-like pallor" on their faces, "shrunken and ghastly white." The "Boys of '98" were marked with a unique badge, the effects of the pestilential fevers of Cuba: "sunken cheek-bones and emaciated forms."

Because these were America's veterans, and because they had come home less than whole or unable to fend for themselves, questions immediately arose about their care. What was to be done for them? Who would do it? This was the starting point for the Veterans of Foreign Wars of the United States (VFW). The VFW was begun by public-spirited (individuals) who understood the terrible injustice done to our returning veterans when they were not given adequate health care and other forms of life-sustaining assistance.

The organization pledged, never again would the veterans of our foreign wars have to scramble to find the care and support they needed.

The VFW mandate would be put to the test only a few years later with the dawning of World War I. Trench warfare was the newest strategy devised for maintaining a military position. This type of warfare was savage and destructive beyond belief. There was no extensive prior experience with this form of warfare, so the horrible effects were not anticipated. Hundreds of thousands of soldiers were "sitting ducks" to fatal diseases and enemy fire falling into the trenches.

The VFW went to work immediately to make sure that the government provided proper medical care and financial assistance for the GIs trying to recuperate from the horrid battle conditions they had endured.

World War II brought new challenges in two theaters: Europe and the Pacific. One calm Sunday morning, the peace at Pearl Harbor was transformed into a blood-bath, bringing America irrevocably into the war and changing the world forever.

In the course of the war, more than 408,306

Americans lost their lives, and another 670,846 were wounded. The sheer magnitude of these casualties called for greatly stepped-up efforts to heal the veterans' battle scars. Again, the VFW was at the forefront, pushing to ensure that the needs of *all* the veterans were met.

The battle which perhaps typified the toughness of the American soldier was the Battle of the Bulge. Although the Germans and Allies had roughly equal numbers, overcast skies and an element of surprise had robbed the Allies of air support. As reported in Lee Kennett's book, *G.I.: The American Soldier in World War II,* the course of this fight altered many German thoughts on the tenacity of the American soldier. A German report issued after the Battle of the Bulge called the American soldier a "first-rate, well trained, and often physically superior opponent." The bitter cold had no "decisive effect on his morale." They said that "often units inside strongpoints had to be wiped out in hand-to-hand fighting." The men who showed their mettle in the Battle of the Bulge proved that this would be "a story to be told to the sound of trumpets."

VFW was instrumental in helping veterans by pushing for passage of the GI Bill of Rights, the Servicemen's Readjustment Act of 1944, which had far-reaching effects on the fortunes of American servicemen and women from World War II forward.

The next war abroad took place in Korea, where soldiers encountered extremes of cold and heat. Rice paddies were fertilized with human excrement, and the stench was overwhelming to the American GI. The North Koreans and the Chinese proved to be worthy adversaries, offering the American soldiers little or no relief from the constant threat of battle.

Robert Leckie's *The March to Glory* describes a

gruesome skirmish typical of the Korean War. Wounded soldiers lay everywhere, filling the landscape with bodies. One young private with a wounded foot struggled to get up, grabbed his rifle, and stumbled out into the darkness to fight back. The cold struck him, making him shake from head to foot. "He moved on, sobbing, his socks sodden from blood and pus issuing from broken blisters," Leckie wrote.

He rejoined his comrade, who was spitting blood into the snow. As he hobbled to position, there was a burst of gunfire, and his comrade received a fragment from an exploding grenade, which tore through his mouth. Looking around him, he saw the captain to his left had been killed, and the lieutenant to his right had fallen dead. "Only the wind seemed to lie between the Chinese and North Ridge." In the end, this soldier's life was saved, but the price was high: He had lost both legs.

The next conflict for the American soldier was perhaps the bitterest of all. Vietnam not only caused losses abroad—it also divided the United States into rival camps of protesters and supporters, who shouted slogans at one another and destroyed national morale.

Even veterans benefits for the returning Vietnam soldier were pitiful. Veterans from Korea and World War II had been granted generous educational stipends under the GI Bill, including full tuition, book costs, and $75 a month for living expenses. Vietnam veterans received a *total* of only $75 a month until the provision was changed in 1969, at which time it was raised to $165 a month if the veteran was a full-time student.

Their welcome home could hardly have been less inviting. The GIs were blamed for having participated in the Vietnam War, and were often given a violent, degrading welcome home. In this way, many citizens took out their anger about the war on those who had fought it, rather than those responsible for waging it.

Vietnam veterans faced a host of problems. Not only were their benefits lacking, but the employment situation in America had also deteriorated by the 1970s, making jobs more difficult to find. Added to this were the deep psychological problems of adjusting back into society. The existence of "post-traumatic stress disorder," suffered by as many as 15% of Vietnam veterans, was not even officially acknowledged until 1981.

The Vietnam War added a new dimension to care for disabled vets; highly sophisticated medical technology and efficient emergency evacuation by helicopter now resulted in a far greater survival rate. The heavy use of mines and booby traps in Vietnam increased the number of severely disabled, and immensely increased the incidence of paraplegia and of multiple amputations over previous wars.

Over 150,000 Vietnam veterans were wounded and required hospitalization. Of those, 75,000 were permanently disabled. Many others suffered from exposure to the chemical defoliant Agent Orange. The price of defending the nation and world freedom in this conflict was extremely high, in human and financial terms.

Through all of this, the VFW was there to lend a helping hand to those who needed medical care and other support services. Among the objectives of the Veterans of Foreign Wars was (and still is) to speed the rehabilitation of the nation's disabled veterans. America called its youth to serve in the Armed Forces and entered into an unwritten pact with the departing soldier: guaranteed care second to none for the wounded and injured. This solemn pledge is something we hope those who defend our country can always depend on.

Many Armed Forces expeditions required great dedication and sacrifice to preserve freedom. Intervention in Lebanon resulted in the tragic loss of 267 American lives from a terrorist attack in 1983-1984.

"Operation Just Cause," launched on December 10, 1989, to invade Panama and depose the drug-dealing dictator Manuel Noriega, ended with 330 Americans wounded in action and 23 killed in action.

The U.S. military has held vital positions in Europe and Asia, the Cold War "front," defending those areas from communism for decades. The success of this huge responsibility spread to Operation Desert Storm where the U.S. Army VII Corps from Germany was most feared by the Iraqi Army because "they turned back the Soviets."

Although not specifically a war, the Cold War had its share of casualties as we skirmished in countries around the globe in an attempt to contain the spread of communism.

The recent "Operation Desert Shield/Desert Storm," which galvanized our nation and resulted in a public outpouring of support second only to World War II, successfully repatriated Kuwait, which had been ruthlessly overrun by Iraqi Colonel Saddam Hussein. On the return home of the Desert Storm veterans, America seemed ready once more to embrace them all and show appreciation for the sacrifices they had made. The VFW played a key role as usual, mobilizing volunteer efforts and visiting the troops at the front.

Ours is a heritage of honor, and a willingness to give what it takes to ensure freedom, liberty, individual rights, and human dignity. That is why the men and women who fought to keep us free must never be forgotten.

As America's oldest major veterans organization, the Veterans of Foreign Wars of the United States has achieved a record of service to veterans and country that is second to none. The VFW has fought and will continue to fight to ensure that our government remembers the challenge made to a younger nation by President Abraham Lincoln: "to care for him who shall have borne the battle and for his widow and for his orphan, to do all which may achieve and cherish a just and lasting peace among ourselves and with all nations.''

I

COMING HOME

The thrill of victory passed like electricity through the crowd of 75,000 midwesterners, who were cheering wildly as the returning troops from Desert Storm marched through Kansas City, Missouri. The air was saturated with flags waving and patriotic music playing over loudspeakers.

The parade was followed by welcoming tributes given by Congressional and military leaders. Words of courage, ideals, and hope in the future of our great country acted like a bonding agent on the crowd— welcoming the troops back into the fold of their families and communities. And these words would help the citizens back home realize that we could never take for granted the freedom these brave soldiers had fought to defend.

It was a great day for all Americans, particularly for the 11,000,000 living veterans of America's wars abroad. American citizens had an occasion to openly display their pride in their military men and women.

The Veterans of Foreign War's "Heart of America" rally, held on June 1, 1991 at Richards-Gebaur AFB outside Kansas City, Missouri, was a fitting celebration of the sacrifices made by veterans and their families in *all* of America's wars, not just the Desert Storm victory.

Military men and women keep inspiring events like these in the back of their minds when they await combat in foxholes and bunkers, on land and sea, and in the air in some foreign place thousands of miles from home. They keep going in the face of often desperate odds, hoping and praying that one day they will come home to their loved ones and resume their normal lives.

But, even though coming home brings to mind

parades, joy, smiles, pats on the back, hugs and prayers of thanksgiving, life will never be the same again for most combat veterans of foreign conflicts. Celebrations come and go, but life goes on—quite painfully—for many thousands of maimed and wounded veterans.

For former Marine and Pulitzer Prize-winning author Lewis Puller, Jr., the moment he was wounded will always remain engraved in his memory: "I could see through a haze of pain that my right thumb and little finger were missing, as was most of my left hand, and I could smell the charred flesh.... I could not see the jagged shards of flesh and bone that had only moments before been my legs, and I did not realize until much later that I had been forever set apart from the rest of humanity." Puller's book, *Fortunate Son,* tells the horror of his life after his tour of duty on the battlefields of Vietnam.

For thousands of other wounded soldiers from our past wars, the physical, mental, and spiritual pain will be with them for the rest of their lives.

No organization understands their pain better than the Veterans of Foreign Wars (VFW). "Honoring the dead by helping the living" is not just a catchy phrase, but the solemn mission of this fine organization. VFW works to improve the lives of veterans, their survivors, and families, finding ways to alleviate the trauma and pain suffered by returning veterans and to help them get on with their lives.

VFW has developed many different types of programs to help meet the widely varying needs of America's veterans. To take just two examples, consider the National Veterans Services (NVS) and its Department Service Officers (DSOs), which provide essential assistance to many veterans seeking to receive the entitlements they were promised, and so richly deserve. Each DSO acts as a liaison between the Department of Veterans Affairs (VA) and the individual veteran. DSOs help veterans cut through the maze of bureaucratic obstacles and secure the benefits promised to them.

"With my husband's long illness, I have had many problems with people in doctors' offices, hospitals, insurance companies, Social Security, Medicare, etc., who just don't care about the people they are serving," Helen Hooper of Hazel Park, Michigan, wrote to the VFW about the DSO who helped her. "I cannot express my gratitude enough to someone interested, caring and observant in their job."

As you can imagine, many veterans and surviving spouses simply don't know what benefits they are entitled to receive, nor do they know how they should go about getting them. Older veterans frequently aren't able to go to the DSO's office, so the DSO comes to them via outreach, visiting in hospitals, nursing homes, or in the veterans' own homes. DSOs also provide a much-needed source of moral, spiritual, and emotional support, because there are many times when a "case" takes months to complete.

DSOs stay on top of the progress of their clients' appeals and offer encouragement to the veteran or survivors who may be on the verge of giving up.

One woman complained that "there have been many times since my discharge from the Navy that I did not know where to obtain help and I lost out on benefits I knew I was entitled to. I am pleased that the VFW has service officers who can effectively advocate the concerns of veterans."

A field office of the National Veterans Service is located at VFW's National Headquarters in Kansas City, Missouri, but the NVS National Office is in Washington, D.C. Services provided by the NVS are wide-ranging, and include periodic surveys of VA facilities, assistance in filing claims, job placement, and discharge upgrading.

Hospitalized veterans *must* receive quality care when they are treated in VA facilities. To this end, patients, service chiefs, employees, and even visitors at VA hospitals are personally interviewed when NVS field reps inspect any of the VA facilities throughout the country. The survey results are shared with various agencies and individuals such as the Department of Veterans Affairs, Congressional representatives, and the national and state leadership of the VFW.

NVS also provides assistance with filing claims for disability benefits and retirement pensions. For example, in recent years, filings for Post Traumatic Stress Disorder (PTSD) have escalated. Most of these claims are from veterans of the Korean and Vietnam wars, both men and women.

Other NVS services range from job assistance to discharge upgrading. Treatment for alcohol and drug abuse is coordinated with local Veterans Health Service and Research Administration Centers. A helping hand is also extended to the veterans down on their luck who need temporary shelter and food.

VFW always has its hands full, since the difficult work of "returning home" and reintegrating into day-to-day life in America takes time, sweat, and the efforts of many people.

What do you do, for example, when you return home less than whole—with perhaps a leg or an arm missing?

"Jim" is typical of thousands of American veterans —but he is also one of the luckier ones. He lost his legs in Vietnam, at a time when military medical care was faster, more efficient, and better than it had been in earlier wars. New prosthetic devices were available that had only been a design in someone's head ten years earlier.

Sadly, veterans who lost limbs in World War II came home to find limited rehabilitative help—and no artificial limbs. Organizations such as the Veterans of

Foreign Wars fought long and hard for the passage of public laws which would grant authority to the Veterans Administration (now the Department of Veterans Affairs) to provide prosthetic appliances and clinical services, research, development, distribution, and education programs.

These laws were a major breakthrough in offering assistance to the disabled, and they helped not only veterans but civilians as well. The VA was soon at the forefront of research and technology for prosthetic devices.

Of course, progress is not always smooth, and not everyone reaps the benefits. Because of federal budget cuts or bureaucratic wrangling, there have been times when the proper devices weren't always available for disabled veterans. One young veteran from New York was fitted with an artificial limb that never fit properly. It caused pain and irritation, and eventually left him with an infected stump. Because of the improper fit, the young veteran had to have more of his leg removed.

Horror stories such as these prompted VFW to pressure the Department of Veterans Affairs (VA) to provide state-of-the-art equipment, thus fixing what was, at most, only a temporary problem.

Still, providing the necessary prostheses for the veteran population is not easy. For example, as veterans of World War II and the Korean War get older, the need for prosthetic appliances, including artificial limbs, wheelchairs, aids for the blind, colostomy bags, oxygen equipment, and automobile adaptive equipment will increase dramatically, since most disabilities requiring amputation are now caused by diseases attributed to aging. Of the 100,000 amputations performed each year, 85% are the result of diseases such as diabetes and peripheral vascular disease. But predicting the demand for veterans' health care services is no mean feat.

And, as medical costs continue to increase, aging veterans face constant challenges. As they require more health care, suddenly they find they can't afford it, they don't have sufficient insurance coverage, and they stand a good chance of becoming another "lost name" in the Medicare/Medicaid rolls.

As veterans grow older in the next few years, the problem of providing the proper services will become even more critical. VFW will continue working to ensure that the nation's deserving veterans get the medical care they need.

* * * * *

It sounds like a code name for a spy or secret society. But it's actually a deadly chemical which was used as a defoliant during the Vietnam War—and a modern-day tragedy. Just to take one widely publicized case, Agent Orange permanently altered the lives of three generations of the Zumwalt family.

In the spring of 1969, Navy boats patrolling along Ca Mau Peninsula, South Vietnam, were searching the tributaries of the Mekong River to cut off enemy supply routes. The dense jungle foliage provided natural camouflage for Viet Cong (VC) guerrillas to ambush the Americans coming down the waterways.

Admiral Elmo Zumwalt, Jr., Commander of the inland Navy patrol boats, was faced with a dilemma. Too many lives were being lost to these ambushes. The only available solution seemed to be the chemical defoliant, Agent Orange, which, according to *VFW Magazine*, would "turn lush jungles into barren wasteland where the VC could no longer hide."

Admiral Zumwalt's son, Lt. Elmo Zumwalt III, was commander of one of the Navy patrol boats. Although care was taken not to spray the chemical defoliant while Navy boats were in the area, it was impossible not to come in contact with residues from the defoliant in the river waters and on the locally grown fruits. Lt. Zumwalt soon noticed a rash on his skin, which he thought was caused by the sun.

In the meantime, patrol boat casualties were dropping dramatically as more and more Agent Orange was sprayed. In the technology of war, Agent Orange seemed like a successful new weapon in the American arsenal.

The next step in the Zumwalt tragedy took place back home. Admiral Zumwalt became chief of naval operations in Washington, D.C. A few months later, his son, Lt. Zumwalt, finally boarded the plane at Ton Son Nhut Airport to leave Vietnam. He remarked, "I had an indescribable feeling of exhilaration of relief. . . . I had been very lucky in Vietnam."

Lt. Zumwalt couldn't have imagined what lay ahead. Wanting only to put the horrid conditions and the killing in Vietnam behind him, he eagerly picked up the pieces of his life, continuing his law studies. He married his long-time sweetheart, and they soon became the proud parents of beautiful, healthy Elmo Russell Zumwalt IV.

Within a few months, the mother became alarmed when baby Russell seemed slow to sit up, crawl, and walk. When their toddler entered nursery school, the Zumwalts' fears increased when the teacher noticed his difficulties in learning. Doctors soon diagnosed disabilities.

Around this time, news stories began associating the birth defects of children born of Vietnam veterans with the veterans' exposure to Agent Orange.

Elmo Zumwalt III then learned he had cancer. Vietnamese medical authorities had reported high rates of birth defects and illnesses in locations where Agent Orange had been sprayed. The American military considered most of these reports to be propaganda. But now, more and more Vietnam veterans were claiming a link between Agent Orange and cancers of many varieties. Mr. Zumwalt wondered if his cancer, too, was caused by the defoliant sprayed under his own father's command.

Elmo Zumwalt III fought a long, drawn-out battle with his disease. He lost his life in 1988. In a heroic gesture, however, not once during his illness did he ever blame his father for having ordered the use of Agent Orange in Vietnam, thus possibly bringing on his own son's demise.

Admiral Elmo Zumwalt carries his anguish inside him every day: "It is the first thing I think of when I awake in the morning and the last thing I remember when I go to sleep at night," he told *VFW Magazine*.

Lobbyists with the Veterans of Foreign Wars have been vigorously fighting to resolve the Agent Orange controversy, and to make sure that veterans who have rightful claims against Agent Orange receive some small measure of help and care that they so desperately need. The VFW has been prodding the VA and Congress for immediate action on this matter. There are many casualties of war, such as those caused by Agent Orange, that don't show up for years after the conflict in question. "Atomic veterans" will continue to pay a high price for the atomic age. On August 5, 1945, the 13-kiloton atomic bomb nicknamed "Little Boy" was dropped on Hiroshima. Four days later, "Fat Man" was detonated over Nagasaki. Japan surrendered and World War II was ended.

But there were American prisoners of war (POWs) being held in Nagasaki at the time. Survivors of the Bataan death march and Japanese labor camps were working in steel mills when the bomb hit Hiroshima. All of these POWs were detailed for clean-up duty within hours of the blasts on Nagasaki and Hiroshima.

By mid-September, when it was considered safe for the POWs to be evacuated from Hiroshima and Nagasaki, most of them were sick from radiation poisoning caused by drinking and eating contaminated water and food, breathing radioactive dust, and handling debris.

Meantime, U.S. ships anchored in Nagasaki harbor routinely used the local water supply for their engines as well as for human consumption. More ships arrived daily, and American military personnel spread out across Japan for occupation duty.

American GIs had no reason to believe that drinking the water, eating the food, or working without protective gear would be harmful. (Only a month after the atomic bombs had been dropped, American inspection teams had declared the ground contamination from radioactive materials to be below the hazardous level.) Although many GIs became ill or developed severe rashes, doctors attributed the ailments to other causes. There was not enough medical experience with atomic fallout to link any symptoms to radiation exposure.

And, of course, after the bombs had been dropped on Japan, the rules of conventional warfare were changed forever. American military strategists now believed that the only way to win the arms race was to lead it.

Atomic tests were soon scheduled to be held on the Bikini and Marshall islands. While target ships were dispersed at varying distances, many ground troops were left on the islands and told to face away from the blast to protect their eyes. After the blast, these soldiers would then turn back to watch the mushroom cloud, leaving themselves virtually unprotected during the radioactive rainstorm that followed.

Ships still afloat were then reboarded and decontaminated. The crews scrubbed the decks, often only in T-shirts and shorts. Some then sandblasted the decks, at the same time inhaling radioactive dust. And ships on site pumped irradiated water on board through a crude purification system.

Even though workers with the Atomic Energy Commission (AEC) suspected there were dangers from radiation, the information was not effectively shared with the crews or other servicemen in potentially dangerous areas.

And while American servicemen were exposed to this radiation more than 40 years ago, only in the past few years has the U.S. government begun to recognize the long-term health affects of radiation exposure.

VFW has provided support for legislation concerning atomic veterans. In 1988, Congress passed the Radiation-Exposed Veterans Compensation Act, signed into law by President Ronald Reagan. Amendments to the act have been considered, because it is felt that many inadequacies remain in the law. For example, there are extremely stringent limitations on which diseases qualify and too many restrictions on the latency period allowed in order to receive compensation.

Only 12,664 of the more than 240,000 known atomic veterans have filed claims. Although more are expected to file, it seems clear that many who deserve compensation will never get it. Because servicemen signed an oath of secrecy at the time of the tests, many saw it as their duty to carry that oath with them to their graves—even though they had been destroyed physically and financially by radiation exposure.

Frankly, though, many American citizens expect more of the government whose liberty and freedom these men fought to preserve. As many of the atomic veterans have been known to say: "You'd think they would have warned us!"

Physical infirmities cause some of veterans' problems, but not all. Many veterans are severely scarred emotionally from their experiences in battle. They routinely contend with recurring nightmares of warfare, reliving memories of seeing their buddies blown up and mutilated before their eyes, and wrestling with demons that only those who have served in the "hellhole" of war can explain. These severe traumas most often don't subside with the passage of time, but require professional help to work through the anguish caused by modern warfare.

VFW has led the way in supporting mental health clinics and special in- and out-patient programs in hospitals across the country to deal with these problems. VFW also works closely with the VA's nationwide network of "Vet Centers" across the country. The Vet Centers offer a sanctuary for veterans dealing with the mental aftereffects of war. By detaching them from the VA hospital sites, locating them in downtown areas of cities, and making them blend in with the surrounding stores, these "storefront" Vet Centers are more readily accepted by veterans who still live "behind invisible walls."

Vet Center staff members are instructed to proceed slowly and treat each individual on a personal basis. Counseling is offered for veterans as well as for their spouses and family.

Veterans suffering from post-traumatic stress disorder (PTSD) are encouraged to participate in group sessions. Sharing and talking about combat experiences can help, especially when they realize they are not alone. Knowing that the support is there can make a critical difference to a veteran seeking assistance.

Alcohol and drug rehabilitation programs also work hand-in-hand with the Vet Centers. Since, quite often, the veteran will experience multiple problems simultaneously, these combined programs offer a doorway for the soldier to pass through on his difficult journey home. But because the disorders can be so complicated and deep-rooted, many veterans don't approach that doorway until much later—sometimes up to 20 or more years later.

One Vietnam veteran expressed it to *VFW Magazine* this way: "You're never gonna forget, but you can contain those memories enough that you can put them up on a shelf . . . bad experiences don't have to dominate your life."

Nobody can understand a veteran's struggles as well as another veteran. That is why the men and women of the VFW family have worked tirelessly since the organization's founding in 1899 to *be there* for those who have risked their lives for our country.

Whether it's medical attention, help in getting their long overdue benefits, job placement services, or just a kind word from a fellow veteran, the Veterans of Foreign Wars exists to make sure veterans understand they are *first-class citizens,* deserving of every honor and privilege America gives to its other heroes and distinguished citizens.

II

"MERE SHADOWS OF THEMSELVES": WHY THE VFW BEGAN

It's one of the oldest stories in the world:

"Most of them returned mere shadows of their former selves. The pale faces, the sunken eyes, the staggering gait and the emaciated forms show...the effect of the climate and disease.

"Many of them are wrecks for life, others are candidates for a premature grave and hundreds will require most careful attention and treatment..."

So wrote the Chief Surgeon of U.S. Volunteers, Dr. Nicholas Senn, describing many of the 18,400 "Boys of '98" who fought in Cuba during the Spanish-American War of 1898. This description also rang true of large numbers of the 125,000 who returned a bit later from the war in the Philippines—and, indeed, it could be said of soldiers returning from practically *every* conflict abroad in *every* era.

Disease has always been proven a second deadly enemy, although in an earlier time, the danger was much more distinct and prevalent than it is today. In the Spanish-American War, for example, only 345 Americans died in combat, while some 2,565 army deaths resulted from non-hostile causes. Tropical diseases struck thousands of troops in Cuba, who were returned to the States and quarantined.

Once back home, their condition only worsened. In the early days of the twentieth century, when medical science and hospital facilities were not as advanced or as available as they are now, the scene was grim.

Thousands of veterans contracted additional diseases while laid up in unsanitary Army camps scattered across the United States. Many of these soldiers died in the camps from typhoid fever and dysentery.

In those days, the troops' quarantine camps in the U.S. were woefully inadequate. Shelter was limited; medical care was poor; camp conditions were filthy; there wasn't enough clothing to go around; and food was moldy and rancid. Small wonder that fevers and diseases took a high toll in these unsanitary settings. Pain and suffering were etched on the faces of almost all the veterans. This pathetic sight forced many to wonder, "Will patriots ever be found again to fight another war? How can our nation allow its brave fighting men to starve and die from neglect?"

Today it is easy to take for granted the benefits and services available to our veterans. But at that time, there was no Veterans of Foreign Wars to fight for the rights of the country's newest veterans. Two existing veterans' organizations, the Grand Army of the Republic and the United Confederate Veterans, refused to allow new veterans to join their ranks.

So the "Boys of '98" banded together and created a group that would be an "overseas fighting men's organization to care for the welfare of fellow veterans."

James Romanis and James C. Putnam, vets of the 17th Infantry Regiment, provided the impetus for the new veterans' organization. Returning to Ohio where he worked in a pharmacy, Romanis came into almost daily contact with veterans of the Spanish-American War who were stricken by tropical diseases. In late September of 1899, his compassion for the suffering of his fellow veterans moved him and Putnam to assemble other ex-enlisted men of his regiment and to form a group to care for these veterans' special medical needs.

Their organization, the American Veterans of Foreign Service (AVFS), was formally incorporated the following month, and its first president was Putnam, a veteran of the Spanish-American War as well as the South Dakota Sioux Uprising of 1890-1891. The men pledged "to help one another and to work together for the benefits of our country and for the men who fight for this nation."

Meanwhile, former officers of the VIII Army Corps in the Philippines were organizing a group of veterans from *their* battle zone across the country in Colorado. This became known as the Society of the Army of the Philippines and was initially led by General Irving Hale, leader of the 2nd Brigade, 2nd Division, VIII Corps, in 28 battles against Filipino insurgents.

Out of the humble beginnings of these two organizations grew the organization we now know as the Veterans of Foreign Wars. Its oldest continuous Post, John S. Stewart Post 1 in Denver, Colorado, still exists today.

But there was still no unity to the various veterans groups. In addition to the Ohio and Colorado contingents, three separate groups of veterans from wars and insurrections in the Philippines, Cuba, and China came together in Pennsylvania to form a separate entity called the American Veterans of Foreign Service in 1903.

Two years later, the Ohio and Pennsylvania organizations merged, retaining the AVFS title. The leaders of the various groups soon realized, however, that a unified organization was badly needed in order to meet the needs of the returning veterans.

But the American Veterans of Foreign Service and the Society of the Army of the Philippines did not formally join forces until September 1914 in Pittsburgh, Pennsylvania. A new name for the organization was chosen: the Veterans of Foreign Wars of the United States. At the same time, a Ladies Auxiliary was formed "to help Posts and members of the Veterans of Foreign Wars."

The first VFW Commander-in-Chief, Rice W. Means, wisely laid the foundation for the organization's future scope, stating that the VFW "must be so broad in its provision for eligibility to include every man who has served or in the future will serve in any war in which the United States is engaged."

And war did come again—perhaps sooner than anyone might have expected. World War I, "the Great War, the war to end all wars," erupted with the assassination of Archduke Ferdinand on June 28, 1914 in Sarajevo.

VFW got started the day America entered World War I, vowing that the injustices done to returning veterans of the 1898-1899 conflict would not be repeated. VFW urged the passage of the War Risk Insurance Act of 1917, which laid the foundation for providing full and reasonable benefits to veterans for the future. This law offered financial assistance to servicemen's families as well as medical compensation for veterans.

As America moved into the "Roaring 20s," the federal government created a new agency, the U.S. Veterans Bureau, which was to be the forerunner of the Veterans Administration (VA). Members of the Veterans of Foreign Wars were instrumental in the formation of the Bureau, which would oversee the benefits and pensions of the veteran population.

Another major VFW milestone during this period was the establishment of a World War I bonus, or a 20-year endowment insurance policy that would mature in 1945. This was passed by Congress with strong VFW support.

And, to help widows and orphans of deceased veterans, the VFW helped found a National Home in Eaton Rapids, Michigan. Built in 1925 on land donated by cattle rancher Corey Spencer, the National Home provided a refuge to countless widows and orphans of deceased veterans over the years.

Then, in 1929, VFW leaders undertook an unprecedented expansion of the VFW's stated purpose by sending an 11-man VFW mission to Russia to secure the remains of 86 Doughboys killed in the North Russia campaign of 1918-1919. Valuable lessons were learned from this experience of dealing with the world's first Communist dictatorship.

In a short 20 years, care for America's veterans had come along way! And it would come at least as far in the next two decades, but not until many hurdles were overcome.

VFW's National Headquarters was established in Kansas City, Missouri, in 1930. In 1936, VFW received its Congressional Charter of Incorporation. Membership in the VFW had already reached 200,000.

The dawn of the Great Depression found thousands of World War I veterans selling apples on street corners and living in makeshift shelters under bridges, railroad trestles, or any secluded spot they could find. These war heroes, who had put their lives on the line to defend our nation, were now forced to beg and live their lives on the streets. Their plight caused VFW to push hard for an early payment of the 20-year endowment insurance policy created in the 1920s, due to be paid in 1945. In part because of the VFW's hard work, a 50% payment on the endowment policy was granted by Congress to veterans in 1932. Four years later, the lawmakers approved full payment of the balance in the form of Savings Bonds.

Not only did the Veterans of Foreign Wars push for the concerns and rights of veterans; they were also instrumental in promoting national pride in America's greatness. For example, recognizing the need for a National Anthem, VFW campaigned for the adoption of Francis Scott Key's "Star Spangled Banner." President Herbert Hoover, who had attended a VFW parade in Baltimore, Maryland in 1930, was persuaded to sign a bill that designated the "Star Spangled Banner" as our National Anthem.

The bill became law in 1931.

During the 1930s, VFW placed an increasing emphasis on promoting patriotism in the United States. To counter the Communist May Day parades, an "Americanism Program" had been established as early as 1921. Americanization Day was first celebrated on April 27, 1921; the day was marked with parades and other outward manifestations of pride in the American way.

Meanwhile, though, concerns over internal security as well as the financial needs of World War I veterans dominated the VFW's agenda throughout the 1930s.

A major turning point occurred when economic depression gave way to another devastating global war—World War II. From the outset, VFW led the way in meeting the immense challenges that lay ahead. The VFW ardently supported a comprehensive 10-point Veterans Program, which was submitted to Congress at the peak of the fighting in World War II.

Portions of this proposed 10-point program became reality when President Franklin D. Roosevelt signed the Servicemen's Readjustment Act, commonly known as the GI Bill of Rights, on June 22, 1944. With the GI Bill, veterans could further their education and buy family homes. A grateful nation stood ready to help returning GIs and their families achieve the American dream.

Following World War II, the programs and operations of the Veterans of Foreign Wars grew tremendously. New programs were started and old ones enhanced. Having succeeded in improving programs for returning veterans, VFW began to embark on several community-oriented ventures as well. Youth activities, begun in the 1920s with Boy Scouts, were greatly expanded to include youth sports; these activities became a full-time concern of the VFW in 1945. VFW's Voice of Democracy program, designed to instill patriotism in high school students, got off the ground in 1946.

President Dwight D. Eisenhower underscored the expanded role of the VFW at the dedication of VFW's Washington office in 1960: "The struggle for freedom does not stop when the guns of war cease firing. Nor will it stop as long as freedom is suppressed or threatened anywhere in the world."

Even with the end of the fascist threat in World War II, world freedom could never be taken for granted. A new generation of soldiers would be called to respond to new threats that flared up around the globe in the 1950s and 1960s.

First, there was Korea. On this foreign soil, American GIs found extremes of biting cold and steaming heat. Although many have referred to this war as the "forgotten war," VFW always worked hard to support our "boys." VFW employees worked diligently to ensure that these veterans received the same benefits as those who had fought in World War II.

After Korea, sporadic conflicts occurred which President John F. Kennedy referred to as a "twilight that is neither peace nor war." To take just two cases as examples, in Lebanon in 1958 and the Dominican Republic in 1965, American troops were deployed to put out Cold War brushfires and maintain peace.

And, because *all* of these brave men and women who served in conflicts abroad were entitled to honorable treatment by the government they fought to protect, the creation of the Armed Forces Expeditionary Medal in 1961 was a welcome development, as it opened the door to eligibility for membership in VFW to thousands of new veterans.

The Vietnam War required a large-scale mobilization of manpower: more than 2.6 million Americans served in this conflict. VFW members visited the troops in the field, and worked to counter the morale problems caused by anti-war demonstrations at home. The organization also campaigned for a Vietnam-era GI bill, which was signed into law in 1967.

Despite the VFW's best efforts to protect the rights and reputations of our soldiers in Vietnam, the large number of returning Vietnam veterans were subjected to a gross lack of respect and recognition when they arrived back home, forcing them to deal with numerous problems that previous veterans had not faced.

Among the unique challenges posed by the Vietnam War, the fate of the prisoners of war (POWs) and those missing in action (MIAs) remains a top priority of VFW to this day. This concern has been at the top of VFW's "must" list for two decades. VFW officials continue to make trips to Vietnam to bring pressure to bear on *our* government not to forget these unaccounted-for servicemen who fought, suffered, and sacrificed to defend the freedom of people on the other side of the world.

The VFW was also moving with the changing times of the 1960s and 1970s, although change was only made where it seemed most reasonable and completely justified. The 70-year old rule barring women from membership in VFW was finally voted down in 1978. Almost one-half of the 1.2 million women veterans had served during wartime, making them eligible for VFW membership. Women have been admitted on an equal basis since 1978, and they now serve in many elected Post and Department leadership positions.

At the same time, with the rapid growth of a spectrum of special-interest groups, it became increasingly evident that the VFW needed to have greater direct involvement in the political process. Events such as the "giveaway" of the Panama Canal, the diplomatic recognition of Red China, and attempts to withdraw U.S. troops from South Korea underscored the urgency for political action.

Likewise, in the 1970s and 1980s, the number of members of Congress who could call themselves veterans and who personally understood the needs of their comrades-in-arms dwindled with each election year. To counteract this diminishing representation by veterans in the halls of Congress, VFW formed a Political Action Committee (PAC) in 1979 to deal effectively with the public policy issues confronting the interests of all soldiers who had fought on foreign soil.

The decade of the 1980s was marked by numerous controversies as well as many successes. VFW foresaw the need and supported legislation to fund psychological counseling centers, education benefits, and employment assistance for America's veterans. Much VFW effort was also expended in trying to protect the independent veterans' health-care system, which was frequently under attack by rival interests.

And, while the war had long been over, there was still much to do on behalf of the soldiers who had fought in Vietnam. A priority effort underscored by the VFW involved the building of the Vietnam Veterans Memorial, which brought long-overdue recognition and respect to Vietnam veterans. In addition, the VFW now lobbies on behalf of the Vietnam Women's Memorial Project, which seeks to honor the female military and medical personnel who made heroic sacrifices for their country.

As stated in the previous chapter, VFW employees worked hard to help veterans exposed to Agent Orange, the chemical defoliant used to eradicate enemy cover in Vietnam, and get the compensation they so desperately needed. VFW also investigated all claims, and provided assistance for the many "Atomic veterans," potential victims of radiation exposure during the occupation of Japan and at test sites in Nevada and several Pacific islands after World War II.

And, with the strong endorsement of the VFW, legislation was finally passed to build a Korean War memorial. Today, the VFW is strongly backing a new project to construct a memorial honoring our soldiers killed in World War II, to be located in Washington, D.C. As you can see, efforts to honor America's veterans are continuous at the Veterans of Foreign Wars!

On the government side, promotion of the veterans' viewpoint progressed when the Veterans Administration (VA) was elevated to full cabinet status in 1988. The creation of a new Department of Veterans Affairs now fully recognized the special role of America's 27 million veterans in preserving the peace and freedom we enjoy in our society.

A special Court of Veterans Appeals was also created to handle judicial review of decisions handed down by the VA on veterans' cases.

In the past decade, often called the "era of violent peace," more youthful veterans have joined the ranks of the VFW, since America has been involved in several overseas expeditionary operations. VFW welcomed with open arms the veterans of conflicts in Lebanon, Grenada, and the Persian Gulf escort mission, as well as, of course, those who recently fought so valiantly in the 1991 Operation Desert Storm.

Fulfilling one of its most important objectives, the VFW maintains a constant vigil over foreign affairs and defense policy, especially with regard to the Western Hemisphere. The VFW agenda has made a "priority item" of the recent efforts to desecrate the United States flag. The VFW has been a strong proponent of a constitutional amendment to protect our country's greatest national symbol.

The VFW organization is as broad as it is powerful and effective. Today, VFW Posts can be found all over the globe. Some 10,700 Posts are situated in the 50 states as well as Panama, England, France, Germany, Japan, Korea, Puerto Rico, Taiwan, and Thailand. VFW community programs also stretch across the nation and have a positive influence on millions of Americans.

Among these, VFW sponsors special scholarship funds for deserving students, who are made aware of the special privileges they can receive only in the greatest country in the world!

To make VFW's remarkable achievements possible, members devote *millions* of volunteer hours each year to local activities. They are motivated by the same priorities of "country, community, and camaraderie," set forth by VFW founders almost 100 years ago—the cornerstone concepts of the Veterans of Foreign Wars.

In the words of Past Commander-in-Chief Walter Hogan, spoken on the occasion of the organization's 90th anniversary in 1989:

"The men who returned from Cuba and the Philippines so many years ago to form the Veterans of Foreign Wars could not possibly have known the potential it held for advocating the rights of veterans. But because of their perseverance, America's veterans of today have the best voice possible to advance their well-earned rights."

If we are to remain a strong, free nation with compassion for all humankind, we must work to ensure that those who fought and will fight to preserve our precious freedoms are not forgotten. All the work of the Veterans of Foreign Wars centers on that basic task of honoring America's heroes.

III

THE LITTLE RED FLOWER
THAT MEANS SO MUCH

"In Flanders Fields the poppies blow
Between the crosses, row on row
That mark our place; and in the sky
The larks, still bravely singing, fly
Scarce heard amid the guns below..."

What does this simple poem have to do with an established nationwide organization of veterans?

Written by Colonel John McCrae, this famous poem about World War I provided the inspiration for the VFW's Buddy Poppy program, which has touched the lives of hundreds of thousands of needy veterans over the years.

Shortly after World War I, the VFW began an assistance program for disabled veterans, which quickly grew into an established tradition across the country. The "Flower of Remembrance" is now synonymous with the mission of the Veterans of Foreign Wars.

Here's how it works:

On Memorial Day and Veterans Day, VFW members come out in force to demonstrate the true meaning of caring. In the streets and byways of towns and cities across the nation selling Buddy Poppies, the flower that has come to symbolize a tradition of giving and caring.

Money raised through Buddy Poppy sales is used to support the entire range of VFW services to needy and distressed veterans. Another way to view the success of this program: consider that almost one billion poppies have been sold to the public since the program began some 70 years ago.

What's so special about these poppies?

The VFW Buddy Poppies are very special, both in their materials and the way they are put together. The stems, petals, and labels are manufactured on contract by a company in Kansas City, Missouri. The parts are then sent to 11 VA hospitals around the country, where disabled veterans assemble them into Buddy Poppies and package them for a nominal fee. The Buddy Poppy packets are then shipped to the VFW headquarters in every state for distribution to local VFW Posts.

VFW Post members volunteer to sell the poppies for donations from citizens who wish to help veterans and their families with special needs.

As you might imagine, the biggest day for sales is Memorial Day. Donations vary, but most poppies go for about $1 each. Every dollar makes a difference to the impact the VFW can have in assisting less fortunate veterans and their families.

Buddy Poppy donations provide relief for veterans awaiting approval of their compensation claims . . . or for those just down on their luck. They can help a veteran pay a grocery or fuel bill. Or these donations might fund a Thanksgiving basket or some Christmas goodies, (discreetly delivered) by a VFW volunteer to a veteran's family, who otherwise would not be able to celebrate.

Contributions also go toward making the holidays a bit brighter for veterans in a VA hospital—either by furnishing their hospital ward with a television set or offering the recuperating soldiers small gifts that bring holiday cheer.

All in all, the Buddy Poppy program helps support each and every branch of the VFW's local and national activities.

What makes the Buddy Poppy program a complete success is the unstinting dedication of the field volunteers, as well as the indispensable help of the Ladies Auxiliary.

VFW members firmly believe that "service to country does not end when you trade in your uniform for civilian clothes." In this spirit, the VFW and its Ladies Auxiliary are partners in community service. For almost 80 years, these two groups have worked together on numerous projects and volunteer programs in communities across the country.

Indeed, there would probably not be a Buddy Poppy program or many other important VFW services if it wasn't for the Ladies Auxiliary. The VFW relies heavily on the more than 7,000 Auxiliaries throughout the country and overseas for their invaluable assistance and leadership in a wide range of program areas.

Since its formation in 1914, the Ladies Auxiliary has made outstanding contributions to America's veterans. The Auxiliary was originally composed of female relatives of veterans from the Spanish-American War. Early members served as volunteers in hospitals, where they cared for the disabled or raised money to help destitute veterans and their dependents.

As the Ladies Auxiliary grew in strength and numbers, it created its own set of programs, at the same time continuing to assist with virtually every VFW program. For example, the Auxiliary raises money each year for its *Cancer Aid and Research Fund*. Donations go to cancer treatment centers nationwide and to deserving medical researchers for postdoctoral fellowships. The Auxiliary also helps to offset cancer-related medical expenses for many of its members.

Untold numbers of Auxiliary volunteers take the time to pay visits to hospitalized veterans. Throughout the year, they are busy making quilts, providing home-baked cookies, hosting holiday parties, or assisting patients to do simple things such as write letters or eat their meals.

To promote patriotism in America and raise funds for the upkeep and improvements to America's "Grand

Lady," the Auxiliary puts on a gala birthday celebration each year for the Statue of Liberty. Likewise, Auxiliary members hold an annual National Young American Creative Patriotic Art Competition, with cash prizes given to the top five entries.

On the education front, Auxiliaries sponsor 245 Junior Girl Units and present scholarships to two outstanding college students each year.

In conjunction with the VFW, the Ladies Auxiliary promotes:

- the Voice of Democracy broadcast speech writing program, with scholarships of almost $2 million to winners at every level of competition,

- Community Activities, recognizing Auxiliaries for their outstanding community service, and

- the Buddy Poppy program, selling several million poppies each year, as well as spearheading many of the creative ideas to support this program.

In 1990 alone, Auxiliary members provided more than 21 million hours of volunteer service in support of the many Auxiliary and VFW programs.

Auxiliary members also make important contributions. For example, throughout the United States, you can always find Auxiliary members leading children in the Pledge of Allegiance, passing out American flags, conducting bicycle safety courses, or even taping bicycles with illumination safety stripes.

During holidays, you'll see them supervising pancake breakfasts, dressing up as clowns for Halloween, and acting as Christmas elves to help Santa distribute presents to needy children.

Auxiliary volunteers drive disabled veterans from their homes to VA medical centers, read to hospitalized veterans, and bake cookies and cakes for bake sales.

Their impact is enormous. Each day, you will find members of the Ladies Auxiliary working to make life a bit better and brighter for someone. Like the VFW, a portion of the revenues from Auxiliary programs, events, and the personal efforts of thousands of Auxiliary volunteers is earmarked for the VFW's National Home.

The National Home is a place where there is an abundance of caring. Founded in 1925 in Eaton Rapids, Michigan, on land donated by a local rancher, the National Home is today a village housing more than one hundred children of veterans. It has its own grocery store, library, fire station, chapel, and 36 brick houses.

Every child at the National Home has experienced his or her own personal tragedy—coping with the death of one or both parents, being caught in the middle of a difficult divorce/custody battle, or struggling with parents who can't provide financial support for the child. Almost every kind of family trauma can be found in the histories of the children who live at the National Home.

The National Home is a refuge, a safe, supportive environment for veterans' children in need. At the same time, the children are free to visit their relatives and friends in their own hometown at any time. Parents and friends may also visit the children at the National Home. Schooling is provided in the nearby community for all who need it, and athletics and other extra-curricular activities are encouraged. To help deserving students continue their education, the Home also pays college tuition for those students who maintain a consistently high grade-point average.

To build self-respect and good character in each of these youngsters, they are encouraged to volunteer their services in the National Home community. He or she may serve as a volunteer firefighter, work in the store or library, tutor a younger student, or help maintain the grounds. In this way, these children learn the importance of giving something back to the community.

The director of programs for the National Home, Susan Shoultz, believes that the Home "is such a beautiful memorial to the veterans who gave their lives for their country. We have taken in their families, and given their children a great opportunity to excel, a loving environment so they learn to care for others, and a sense of obligation to give back what they have received."

The National Home is raising some of America's leaders for the next generation. Each of these youngsters has unique talents to offer. Who are some of the Home's shining stars?

There is *Frances*, an associate professor of television/radio/film at Syracuse University. She recently spent time in London and Brussels, Belgium with several of her students.

Sharon is a senior tradesworker at Northern Michigan University, and the campus' locksmith. After earning her bachelor's degree from NMU in the mid 1970s, Sharon was the first woman commissioned in the U.S. Army from the NMU ROTC program. She studied military police operations and attained the rank of captain while completing an eight year commitment in the Army reserves.

Brothers *Wes* and *Warren* are juniors at Ball State University. Wes is majoring in education and plans to teach secondary english and physical education. Warren is majoring in legal administration and would like to attend law school.

At Albion College, *Maydene* is a pre-med student with hopes of becoming an emergency room doctor. Maydene graduated in the top ten of her class and earned three varsity letters in basketball, volleyball and track.

These are just a few examples of the outstanding youngsters who have been given a "second chance" at VFW's National Home. There is no telling where many of these children may have ended up if they had not been given the love and guidance they found in abundance at the Home. Certainly, they might have gone the way of many of today's rootless youth—on drugs, into crime and prostitution, living a life with no prospects and no future.

The children of our veterans deserve the best, and that is why the National Home was established. Parents made tremendous sacrifices so that we all might live peacefully and in accordance with our cherished liberties; it seems only fitting that we show our gratitude to these brave former soldiers by helping their children when their parents are unable to raise them themselves.

The VFW National Home does not receive any government subsidies, but depends solely on the generosity of its donors. Naturally, since it is a thriving community, there is always a need for something extra, so the National Home is constantly seeking more funding support. Monies for food, clothing, utilities, staff, medical care, and transportation come from the sale of National Home Seals and Buddy Poppies, life memberships, general contributions, and the investment earnings of the endowment fund. Of course, private donations also make a tremendous difference in the level of services provided at the National Home.

Another example of the VFW's continuing service to veterans and their families is the "Operation Hometown" program, a source of tremendous pride for every VFW and Ladies Auxiliary member. When President Bush ordered our troops to be sent on Operation Desert Shield in August 1990, VFW Posts and Auxiliaries throughout the nation quickly mobilized to provide goods and services that would boost the morale of our troops preparing for battle on the remote desert sands of the Middle East.

Twenty-three private companies helped support VFW's efforts with donations of money and materials. Funds paid for the transport of items to airlift and shipping points, and for packing, boxes, postage, and printing.

Through the efforts of "Operation Hometown," some 100,000 packages were distributed to the troops. The VFW flew more than 10,000 holiday packages to soldiers, so they might enjoy a bit of Thanksgiving and Christmas. Another 600 packages were personally delivered by Kansas Senator Robert Dole on his trip to the Mideast.

The first 50,000 boxes were packed by the disabled working in Kansas City. The second 50,000 were packed under the Compensated Work Therapy Program at the VA Medical Center in Topeka, Kansas—taking advantage of the services of veterans exclusively. Here was a true example of veterans helping their fellow soldiers!

Hundreds of Posts and Auxiliaries responded with additional local programs of their own, from letter-writing campaigns to cookie and candy drives. Assistance offered to the troops' families back home helped the families cope with the absence of one and sometimes two military parents. Needless to say, the VFW's family support also helped ease the concerns of soldiers halfway across the globe who worried about their families back home.

In many cases, a broken-down car was repaired so the wife could continue going to work. Babysitters were provided to give relief to families left with only one parent. Hotlines were set up for the children to have someone to talk to—helping calm their fears and even helping them with their homework.

Volunteers flocked by the thousands to help with "Operation Hometown." Everyone wanted to be a part of this important effort to let our soldiers of Operation Desert Shield/Storm know that the people back home cared—and that their families would be taken care of.

The response from the trooops was enthusiastic and extremely grateful. One wrote to the VFW: "I am proud to be a veteran and honored to be a member of the

VFW which is supporting the American military over here."

Another responded: "It's absolutely wonderful that the folks back home are supporting us. When I get back home to Georgia, I am hoping to become a member of our (VFW) Post there."

A sergeant spoke for many when he wrote, "It's pretty hard being away from home, especially during the holidays, but it sure does make me feel better hearing from people who know exactly what I'm going through. Thank you!"

Operation Hometown is yet another example of the boundless goodwill shown by the thousands of VFW and Ladies Auxiliary members. It is a testament to their lasting commitment to serve, which doesn't end when their tours of duty have ended. Thanks to them, our soldiers who fight abroad can serve with singleminded purpose, knowing that wives, husbands, and children are being supported back home.

That's a good example of the whole VFW philosophy, a creed which is summed up by a single red flower that has come to stand for the comradeship—the VFW Buddy Poppy, just one symbol of all the caring VFW members have for their less fortunate fellows.

IV

THE WAR TO END ALL WARS

They called it "the very threshold of Hell."

American Doughboys, young men sent to defend freedom during the First World War, experienced the horror of brutal, bloody trench warfare first-hand. No war is pleasant, but no previous war had ever seen such vicious fighting practices prevail, killing millions of soldiers in so short a time.

Both sides in this bloody conflict used trench warfare as their military strategy. Front-line trenches, dug into the earth, stretched some 15,000 miles on the Allied side alone. These trenches formed the first defense against attacks from across a narrow "no-man's land," 200 to 500 yards separating the trenches of the opposing armies.

One young soldier, describing his front-line experiences in Belgium, said that because most of the Belgium countryside was so low relative to sea level, it was impossible to dig more than two to four feet underground before you hit water. In many of these shallow trenches, soldiers would lie or crouch for hours on end in extremely cramped positions—often dying in those same contorted positions, when enemy fire hit them.

After the trenches were dug, they were fortified in front with sandbags and barbed-wire entanglements. The floors of the trenches were covered with duckboard, which kept the soldiers' feet dry provided it didn't rain. Shallow dugouts were made in the back wall of the trench, from which soldiers could look into "no-man's land" without the danger of being seen by the enemy.

Writing about one confrontation in his war memoirs, *Fighting Soldier, The AEF in 1918*, Joseph Douglas

Lawrence remembers a constant barrage of screeching and exploding shells, which threw up blinding, choking clouds of earth. "Fragments of shells whined over the top of our trench and clods fell in on us from the parapet. We crouched close to the front side of the trench while the earth poured down on us." In the deafening roar of the exploding shells, one man was hit and his body instantly covered with dirt.

Before they could recover from one shell, another would come...and then another. The Germans' shelling would continue for a solid half hour and then quiet down.

Most soldiers stayed in the trenches for an average of four to seven days. Battle was waged not only against the enemy—there was also the constant struggle with nature. The prime enemies here were water and mud. Water-filled shell holes in the trenches quickly became death traps, sucking wounded men under and drowning them. The never-ending dampness and cold caused "trench foot," as well as fatal respiratory diseases.

Filth was a constant companion. The stench of decaying bodies was more than even the most hardened veterans could bear. Rats brought "Weil's disease," an infectious jaundice. Lice transmitted "trench fever," and summer flies brought all types of diseases. Itch mites caused "scabies," and nits infested soldiers' hair.

After several years of siege and bloodbath, the British and French troops were still stoical and courageous—but exhausted, relieved when American forces joined the fray in 1917.

From the first, President Woodrow Wilson had been reluctant to commit his country to war. American public opinion was not unanimous, (with) many supporting isolationism and pacifism. However, by the time American diplomatic relations were severed with Germany in February 1917, patriotic fervor had swept the country like wildfire. One symbol of this was the short, moving letter former President Theodore Roosevelt wrote to the Secretary of State (for War):

"Sir, if my life and that of my four sons can be of any help in the defense of the country, please consider them as being placed at your disposal. . . ."

The State of Utah sent a telegram to the federal government in Washington, D.C., stating that "Ten thousand Navajo Indians are ready to go to war and fight to the death against Germany."

And many of the Germans living in the United States at the time rushed to obtain naturalization papers— and, if called, to fight for their new homeland.

Even former President Taft, who was then chairman of the League to Enforce Peace, called the nation to arms with the conscience-goading question: "Are we going to remain in our rocking-chairs while the conflict rages at our doors?"

After the February break in diplomatic relations, several American ships were sunk by German submarines. The incident which directly prompted the President's decision to go to war was the "Zimmermann telegram," which was intercepted and deciphered by the British Secret Service. Dr. Arthur Zimmermann, the German Foreign Secretary, in an effort to capitalize on the border incidents between the United States and Mexico, sent a telegram to the Mexican government proposing an alliance between Mexico and Germany which offered considerable financial incentives for the Mexicans. In return for their cooperation, for example, the telegram spelled out that Mexico would be granted annexation rights by the German government to the American states of Texas, New Mexico, and Arizona.

President Wilson addressed Congress on the night of April 2, 1917. In his speech he said in a clear, precise voice:

"There is one choice we cannot make, we are incapable of making; we will not choose the path of submission and suffer the most sacred rights of our nation and our people to be ignored or violated . . .

"It is a fearful thing to lead this great, peaceful people into war—into the most terrible and disastrous of all wars, civilization itself seeming to be in the balance.

"But the right is more precious than peace, and we shall fight for the things which we have always carried nearest our hearts—for democracy, for the right of those who submit to authority to have a voice in their own government, for the rights and liberties of small nations, for a universal dominion of right by such a concert of free peoples as shall bring peace and safety to all nations and make the world itself at last free . . . "

On April 6, 1917, the U.S. Congress declared war on Germany by a vote of 373 to 50. After months of waiting, America had entered this greatest of wars.

Our American soldiers had no doubts who the enemy was, what they were fighting for, and what the outcome would be. The Doughboys were eager to "eradicate the Hun from Europe." They believed they were waging war for God and country. These fresh, brave American soldiers were determined to see to it that right won over might.

They came striding in with a flush of youthful vigor and pride. At times, they were even felt to be a bit naive. But this naivete served them well. By pledging to make the world safe for democracy, and by believing that if the ultimate sacrifice was necessary, it was for a worthy cause. They were able to fight for good over evil with unequalled vigor.

The French declared 1917 the coldest winter in years, if not for all of recorded history. American soldiers marched on roads in shoes that were totally inadequate, often lasting only a few days. Many went barefoot—as could be seen by the bloody footprints they left in the snow.

It was at this point that General John J. Pershing, realizing that the only possibility of winning the war lay in a fundamental change of strategy, began to take the war out of the trenches and into the air. Of course, with the change came a whole new crop of problems.

The men in the air forces had great difficulty keeping their engines, cooled by water, from freezing in the sub-zero temperatures. Water and oil had to be heated before being put into a plane's engine, often causing inconvenient delays. Primitive fighter planes provided little protection for pilots and crews from the elements. Pilots flying at high altitudes often found their noses and faces frozen.

American pilots were quite adept at flying planes but had no experience in combat. It was awhile before American pilots were in full action, making the hits that counted. Of course, with the learning curve came many casualties.

One young soldier, describing the death of his brother, says his brother's plane had been forced to land due to engine trouble. As he tried to land, the plane bounced on the runway and the back part of the fuse-lage broke, killing him instantly. The soldier laments: "My only brother, a young man, just twenty-two. He was everything a brother should be. Why? It should have been me. The funeral was held the next day."

Problems with weaponry also plagued the Allies. On-board machine guns stuck when too much oil was left on them. Oil would gum up in the cold, and the metal broke at the seams when temperatures fell too low.

As the Allies changed their tactics, the enemy tried to keep up by shifting their own strategies. By April 1918, the Germans had developed a long-range cannon that could shoot seventy-two miles. With it, they realized they could hit Paris. So when they first fired this cannon, the Allied forces looked into the skies, thinking they would spot the airplanes that had dropped these projectiles. Eventually, they were able to determine the location of the gun through projectile measurement, but the Germans had camouflaged this cannon so well that airplanes couldn't find and destroy it.

Another wartime innovation—poison gas—led to new and terrible ways of wounding and killing soldiers. The Doughboy was the first American soldier ever to encounter poison gas on the battlefield. Chlorine, mustard, and phosgene gases were used. Of the three, mustard gas was the most deadly.

The American fighting men, or Doughboys, won the praise of both friends and foes. (They were called "Doughboys,"—in a corruption of the word "adobe," —a term coined during the Mexican War (1846-48) to describe foot soldiers who often became caked with soft, white, powdery dirt while marching behind the cavalry).

The American Expeditionary Force was proud of its might and the principles for which it fought. They helped win this tremendous conflict with honor. Because of their deep affection for one another, they were willing to risk everything for victory—fighting hand to hand and standing tall under artillery fire. Their heroic spirit shone through the dust and debris of the battlefield.

Finally, with the participation of the American soldiers, the tide began to turn for the Allies. In the Second Battle of the Marne, on July 15, 1918, the Allies found they had a distinct advantage, both in surprise and numbers. Allied tanks and the combined air forces proved overwhelming to the German ranks.

The losses during the Second Battle of the Marne were heavy on both sides. One of those who fought valiantly and was killed in action was Quentin Roosevelt, son of former President Theodore Roosevelt. A fighting ace, he was shot down in one of the daily dog-fights with German pilots.

Through September and October of 1918, the Allies pressed forward with their attacks. The German armies were steadily disintegrating and the fronts steadily crumbling. Victory for the Allies seemed assured before the end of the year.

Finally, the Germans capitulated and, on November 11, 1918, the Armistice was signed. In Paris, a cannon announcing peace was fired, and church bells began to ring.

In the trenches, however, all was quiet. There was relief, expressed as an eerie silence all along the Western front. It was hard for the soldiers to comprehend that the end of four years of horror had finally arrived!

Marshal Foch, the French commander and head of the Allied troops, addressed his victorious armies this way:

"You have won the greatest battle in history and saved the most sacred cause, the Liberty of the world.

"Be proud. You have pinned immortal glory to your flags.

"Posterity will always remember you gratefully."

Almost 50 million men from thirty nations served in World War I. Of those, 10 million lost their lives in combat. Another 20 million were wounded or crippled.

Ultimately, World War I served as a violent transition which carried the United States into a new era of realism. The American boys who left home eager to serve returned as men, changed forever. But that stark realism was cushioned by the open arms and helping hands of the Veterans of Foreign Wars. VFW volunteers fought for adequate compensation and medical care for the 204,000 wounded from shot and shell in the trenches, the tens of thousands exposed to mustard gas, and the many racked by diseases such as cholera, "trench foot," and respiratory illness.

Disabled Doughboys, who were cynically called "used-up boys," provided a powerful base of experience and the impetus VFW needed to pursue its fight for the rights of discharged servicemen throughout the 1920s and 1930s.

Particular VFW achievements during this period include pushing through the War Risk Insurance Act of 1917, which provided compensation benefits and vocational training for disabled veterans, and pension bills for veterans, widows and orphans of World War I. VFW was also instrumental in passage of the World War Veterans Act of 1924, a bill creating regional Veterans Bureau offices and, by 1930, the Veterans Administration itself.

The challenges faced by the VFW in assisting our returning heroes were many and varied. It wasn't easy trying to cope with new problems which could not have been foreseen—particularly events such as the Great Depression and emotional problems caused by the new technologies of war.

With the Great Depression close on the heels of the war, as more and more homeless veterans began to appear on street corners across the nation, the VFW fought to supply veterans with their rightful bonuses, so that they might be able to eke out some kind of normal life.

These veterans' hardships did not end when they returned home; in fact, their problems were also discovered to be much deeper-rooted than just the run-of-the-mill financial or economic difficulties.

Their experiences in the trenches had been a unique nightmare, creating powerful, haunting images that many would relive back home every single moment of every day of their lives. These men dealt constantly with their post-war trauma and old wounds that wouldn't go away. Many developed what is now called "war neurosis," or an emotional disorder resulting from the horrors of war.

Trench warfare had been very conducive to these nervous disorders, which were found to be much more prevalent among men who remained inactive during shelling or immobilized in trenches during combat. An hour or two of this kind of shelling over their heads and all around them was more than most men could stand. They would listen as each shell approached, wondering how close it would come and whether this one would be the one that hit them where they lay. The tension of remaining immobile was much more difficult to deal with than being able to carry out a soldier's duties while on the move.

Ending the fighting only meant the beginning of the flashbacks of horror. For many, war neurosis didn't develop for years after they returned home. It lay smoldering in their unconscious minds long before it became apparent or was recognized.

There were many reasons why the symptoms of this war neurosis often took on forms quite different from what it really was. As a defense against the horrors of war, men who had served in such unnatural conditions as the trenches often developed overly idealistic images of home. Then, upon returning home, they found it too radically different from the images they had created. Incredibly, these men often began longing for the comradeship of the front again.

They now idealized the support and understanding they had received at the front from their fellow soldiers.

For others, the aggressions bottled up in war found other targets at home. All of these men required special attention, which they were able to find through the kind services of VFW volunteers.

Five shell shock centers were set up in the United States to treat soldiers suffering from symptoms of shell shock or combat fatigue, a psychoneurotic condition characterized by anxiety, irritability, and depression. The VFW helped veterans get the much-needed treatment they deserved at these centers. In addition, the VFW pushed the government to recognize war neurosis as a condition caused by the horrible environment of trench warfare, and therefore deserving of special support.

VFW also fought for proper treatment and compensation for soldiers exposed to poison gases—namely, chlorine, phosgene, and mustard gases. There were approximately 58,000 American casualties due to these gases, including 2,000 deaths.

Even the returning soldiers who didn't suffer from some form of physical or mental illness had their share of difficulties to cope with. For one, there was the natural forgetfulness of the citizens on whose behalf they had fought. This has been true in all ages and for all peoples: Once the fighting is over and things have returned to normal, the heroic soldier promptly goes to the back of people's minds.

That is precisely what happened in 1918. Hailed as heroes on their return home, some 200,000 Doughboys marched in 450 parades held across America. But once the euphoria had subsided, once the newspaper stories had yellowed and the festoons and ticker tape were swept off of America's streets, these veterans experienced a sudden reversal in the eyes of the public.

VFW understood the neglect they might eventually feel, and hence VFW volunteers worked hard to make these veterans feel welcome. Membership in the VFW organization increased dramatically, offering help and a sense of fellowship to thousands of Doughboys.

Some of the more famous men who joined around this time were former President Theodore Roosevelt and future President Harry S Truman, a veteran of the 35th Division's 129th Artillery. General of the Armies John J. Pershing, member of Lawton Post 27 in the Philippines, was named Honorary Commander-in-Chief of the Veterans of Foreign Wars on a visit to Kansas City, site of the national headquarters.

America's Doughboys made tremendous sacrifices for the cause of world freedom in the First World War. They lit a flame which free men and women could continue to carry high. In the words of their former commander, General Pershing:

"In their devotion, their valor, and in the loyal fulfillment of their obligations, the officers and men of the American Expeditionary Forces have left a heritage of which those who follow may ever be proud."

For this reason alone, it was only fitting that the VFW help them fit back into the society they had left. VFW staff and volunteers worked tirelessly to see that veterans received their much-deserved compensations and pensions; the VFW also negotiated with the government to make sure veterans were given prompt, proper medical treatment to restore them to health.

In essence, the VFW was fighting for nothing more than to give these men some small token of support and appreciation in return for the hardships they had endured in defense of our nation while serving on "the very threshold of Hell."

V

WORLD WAR II:
A NATION UNITED

On Sunday, December 7, 1941, the calm beauty of the Hawaii sunrise was shattered by the attack of Japanese bombers on the U.S. Naval Base at Pearl Harbor. It was a day that changed our world forever—the day that forced our participation in World War II. Having hoped for peace, the U.S. was, in a flash, engaged in war.

Within the first two hours of our involvement, the United States lost eight battleships, three cruisers, four other vessels, 188 airplanes, and several vital shore installations. More than 2,000 soldiers and sailors died, and 1,000 were injured.

Those who survived had overwhelming stories to tell. It was truly miraculous that anyone could have survived the surprise attack.

"I had just finished breakfast and was shaving when I heard airplanes racing outside my window," remembered Donald Ross, a young machinist mate on the battleship *Nevada,* anchored in Pearl Harbor. Looking out the window, he saw "three Japanese Zeroes screaming over the east side of Ford Island firing hot flames from their guns." Ross then heard a big explosion, and he rushed to the Forward Generator Room."Within three minutes, the *Nevada* was on full combat condition ZED or general quarters."

Bombs were destroying planes still on the runway, and gas tanks were blowing up everywhere. The *Nevada* was blasted by a torpedo, which blew a hole 60 feet long and 18 feet below the water line on the port bow near Turret Two. This hole was only 40 feet from the Forward Generator Room, and the battleship was rapidly shifting in the water. Ross knew the generators had to be switched to the Rear Dynamo Room as quickly as possible in order to save the ships.

But before Ross could move, a second group of Japanese bombers hit the battleship. More water came gushing in, and the pumps couldn't work fast enough to offset the incoming flow. Yet another bomb found its mark, blinding Ross in his left eye. He momentarily lost consciousness, then recovered and ordered his men to evacuate immediately. Just in time, too—the smoke was intense; the temperature in the Forward Generator Room had risen to 140 degrees.

All alone, Ross struggled to pull the switch that would alternate the generators in time to save the *Nevada*. In the dense heat, smoke, and almost total darkness, this heroic sailor fought to switch off to the rear generators, just managing to accomplish his mission before he fell unconscious.

An electrician nearby heard his faint cry, "God help me," and rushed to his rescue. He found Ross already unconscious and not breathing. By applying artificial respiration, the electrician brought Ross back to life, but just as he began to breathe again, Ross remembered that "the exhaust in the forward condensers had not been secured," which could have resulted in a terrible explosion.

He fought his way back through the black smoke and complete darkness, found the pipe cut-off valve, and turned it just in time to avoid explosion.

When the Japanese attack was over, the *Battleship Nevada* was badly damaged but still afloat. Although 57 brave sailors onboard died, many more would have been lost—along with the Nevada itself—if not for the valiant actions of machinist Donald Ross. As he remembered that fatal morning, Ross reflected:

"I didn't think about fear. I was frightened, but the fear didn't control me. The most important thing was my men and the ship. These were more important to me than my own life."

This story is typical of the young men who fought in World War II. Their complete sense of duty, dedication, and respect for their fellow soldiers formed the motive and basis of one brave deed after another.

World War II was a "total war," one in which every man, woman, and child on the face of the earth played a part. Although the United States had fought in World War I, it was scant preparation for the all-consuming military experience of World War II. A war carried on in two theaters, with armed forces engaged in combat around the globe—not for just a few months, but for nearly four years—was unprecedented in human history. The conflict extended from the soldier on the front lines to the citizen in the remotest town.

In World War II, the causes of the conflict were clear; the necessity of war was unquestionable; the execution was well managed; the end was definitive. A trio of evil, ruthless tyrants attacked a benevolent, united force of free, democratic nations. Nazism and Fascism were founded on a hate for and a desire to eradicate all non-Aryan races. The final aim of these pernicious ideologies was nothing short of total domination of the world. Therefore, the resulting aggression of Germany and her allies had to be fiercely challenged and ultimately defeated.

Americans were *almost* ready for the war when the attack on Pearl Harbor came. They had vigorously debated their possible participation before the war had begun. Once the United States had entered the fray, Americans united as never before in the face of the ugly threat of world oppression. Since the forces of aggression in World War II truly formed a world conspiracy, Americans knew they must meet the challenge.

With the Great Depression now at an end, the industrial expansion boomed as never before in support of the wartime effort. In every corner of the nation, people were mobilizing for a variety of necessary tasks. As the men left for the battlefront, women replaced them on assembly lines and performed other vital tasks in the work force. Women took over key positions in the production of armaments, equipment, and supplies, crucial to the fighting and a determining factor in the ultimate Allied victory.

Late in the war, Soviet leader Joseph Stalin paid tribute to the American men and women at home when he offered a toast to President Roosevelt with the words: "To American production, without which the war would have been lost."

America's military leaders were well aware of the critical role of a concerted civilian effort at home in support of the soldiers abroad. The armed forces printed and distributed official posters exhorting civilians to work hard on behalf of the troops. On one of these posters, the newfound importance of America's working women was immortalized in the popular image of "Rosie the Riveter."

World War II propelled the Veterans of Foreign Wars into action on two fronts—in helping America to win the war and in providing for the veterans once the war was over.

An *ad hoc* VFW War Service Commission was formed, whose first order of business was to approve the purchase of 15 training planes for the government. No sooner had war been declared than the VFW offered its services to the director of Civil Defense.

Under the director's auspices, the VFW was given primary responsibility for organizing auxiliary police and firefighting forces. VFW Post homes became centers for training new recruits.

In another effort to promote war-preparedness, the VFW and the American Legion were asked by the federal government to head up a nationwide program designed to help Americans—especially young men likely to be drafted—improve their physical fitness. Likewise, a VFW-sponsored literacy campaign was aimed at a million men throughout the nation who had been rejected for the draft because they couldn't read.

In addition, the VFW launched an education campaign to strengthen democratic feelings and principles, to bolster basic American values, and to expose subversive elements within the borders of the United States. In 1940, the VFW launched a 15-minute radio program, "Speak up for Democracy," which reached 485 radio stations up to the final days of the war. VFW informational booklets were prepared on a variety of important patriotic subjects, ranging from lessons on how to handle the American flag to the warning signs displayed by subversive elements in the United States.

A home-grown VFW campaign referred to as "Rumor Swatting" cautioned against spreading stories which might include information that would aid the enemy. The VFW also maintained close contact with the FBI, in order to coordinate efforts to guard against activities of enemy agents and to report possible domestic acts of sabotage or espionage.

To engender strong support for the war, VFW distributed thousands of inspirational posters to VFW Posts and local newspapers throughout the country. In a parallel effort, the Ladies Auxiliary distributed 180,000 posters, encouraging Americans at home to write letters of support to service members fighting far from their home towns.

The VFW organized a steady stream of war bond campaigns and fund-raising efforts to buy Army ambulances. VFW Post members diligently gave blood to hospitals and visited returning soldiers who had been disabled in combat, bringing them gifts of books and other personal items of cheer while they recuperated.

Even before the war had ended, plans were formed to

provide assistance to the "new" veterans when they returned home. High on the list of VFW priorities was the restructuring of the National Rehabilitation Service, which would help hundreds of thousands of veterans who needed special medical and physical therapy services.

The Costs of War: The Soldiers' Stories

By mid-1943, the American and Allied troops had met with considerable success in halting the Axis advance in both the Europe and Pacific arenas. Over the next two years, the Allies would seize the offensive and launch a series of powerful, well-coordinated campaigns which would carry them forward to complete victory.

But, up until this time, the Allies had been overshadowed by the Fascist peril—not only in Europe and the Pacific, either. From his nearby vantage point, Italian dictator Benito Mussolini had watched his Axis partner Adolf Hitler overrun one country after another across Europe. Late in the summer of 1940, Mussolini decided to mount his own campaign in North Africa, sending Italian troops across the Western Desert in Libya in order to invade British-controlled Egypt.

But war in the desert turned out to be very different from war on the European continent. The lack of distinctive landmarks or "front lines" made it more akin to fighting sea battles. With more experience fighting in the desert, the British troops managed handily to overcome the Italians, forcing Hitler to dispatch General Erwin Rommel, commander of the newly formed *Afrika Korps,* to North Africa in March 1941.

A new configuration of forces was deployed in the desert combat. On the one hand, there was Rommel, who soon acquired the name of the "Desert Fox" for his cunning and brilliant military maneuvers. On the other side, British Lieutenant General Bernard Law Montgomery—"Monty" to his men—became commander of the Eighth Army in North Africa, breathing new leadership and new confidence into his desert troops. While the toll was high on both sides, the British soon forced Rommel to retreat westward.

With the British success came a new, revived Allied offensive. "Operation Torch," made up of over 107,000 troops, three-fourths of them Americans and one-quarter British, was an amphibious operation on a scale never before attempted. The massed troops were deployed first to capture Casablanca in Morocco. They would land from the sea, then march eastward into Tunisia, seizing the major ports nearest the Axis bases in southern Europe.

General Dwight D. Eisenhower was Commander-in-Chief of "Operation Torch." It got off to a promising start, but then had to be postponed until springtime due to bad weather and difficult terrain conditions. Eventually, after a series of drawn-out, bloody battles, North Africa was secured by the Allies.

From their vantage point in Libya and Egypt, the Allied forces then crossed the Mediterranean into Italy, first assaulting Sicily on July 9–10, 1943. By September 9, Mussolini was brought to his knees, unconditionally surrendering his country.

But the taking of Italy was not without bloodshed. On the road to Rome, some 40,000 Allied soldiers were killed, wounded or missing. The Germans lost 38,000 men in the bitter fighting. One of the worst days of carnage during the Italian campaign had taken place at Anzio. There, a squadron of beleaguered GIs, severely outnumbered, dug into their positions, refusing to budge. Day in and day out, they fought at close range with the enemy. By sheer force of will, courage, and determination, the Americans pulled through, although not without heavy losses.

By now, though, there was no doubt that the fortunes of war had turned for the Allied forces. Victory seemed virtually assured. Early in 1944, American and British bombers were attacking industrial installations in Germany. Massive bombing had already taken place in several German cities, notably Dresden, causing severe damage.

In Great Britain, the Allies had been gathering an enormous invasion force for almost two years, destined to be deployed on the European continent. The bombing of Germany helped clear the way for this great Allied landing on the beaches of northern France in the spring of 1944. The invasion began on the morning of June 6, 1944, on what became known as "D-Day." Three million troops and perhaps the greatest array of armaments and naval vessels ever assembled landed on the coast of Normandy. While the Germans were anticipating such an attack by Allied forces, they had always believed it would come from the Atlantic Coast, so they were not prepared for the Normandy invasion.

Those who witnessed or participated in the landing could scarcely believe their eyes—even if they knew perfectly well what was happening. Suddenly, at dawn, the English Channel was full of ships and the air filled with the rumbling roar of gunfire.

The landing at Utah Beach was considered a resounding success, even though 197 soldiers were reported dead and 60 missing, presumed drowned.

Omaha Beach, on the other hand, was the bloodiest battle of D-Day. Its name would be enshrined in American military annals alongside such scenes of carnage as Antietam or Gettysburg. It was at Omaha Beach that the Germans came closest to forcing the Allied invaders back to sea.

The beach, which featured 100-foot cliffs at each end with a seawall at the back, was well-fortified by the Germans. Four exits off the beach went through heavily wooded ravines to fortified villages. Between the tidelines, the beach was thick with mined obstacles, and every inch was pre-sighted for dug-in Germany artillery.

As the ramps of the landing craft were lowered and the troops rushed out, a German machine gunner opened up on the Americans from one end of their line to the other. Howitzer shells exploded among the men on the beach and the first troops off the boats ran directly into a wall of fire. The men just crumpled and fell face down into the sand and water. When the tide came in later that day, the bodies strewn along the pebble embankment formed a belt more than seven yards wide.

By midmorning, however, some 200 Americans had made it through the German line of fire, and they were a sufficient force to fight off a German counterattack. Reinforcements were called in, and Navy destroyers approached the beach head in order to fire salvoes at the Germans. With victories assured at other spots along the coast, the Allies were able to hold their own at Omaha Beach.

Within a week's time, the German forces were forced to beat a hasty retreat from all points along the Normandy coast. Even so, Allied progress inland from the coast remained slow for the next few weeks.

Late in July, the Allies chalked up a well-deserved victory at the Battle of Saint-Lo, an important turning point in the campaign to restore France to the French people. After four years of German occupation, Paris was finally liberated on August 25, 1944. By the middle of September, the Germans had been pushed out of France and Belgium almost entirely.

But the German forces re-grouped and presented a solid front along the Rhine River. In terrible weather—

rain, cold, and snow—the Germans struck in desperation along a fifty-mile front in the Ardennes Forest. The battle that ensued there, beginning on December 16, 1944, is commonly known as the Battle of the Bulge.

Americans who fought in this battle remember the bitter cold, the frostbite, and the "tree bursts," or artillery shells that exploded on tree trunks and branches, raining death over a wide area below. There was little defense against these explosions, since throwing yourself on the ground only made you a "sitting duck" for a tree burst.

With danger lurking everywhere, the Battle of the Bulge raged for six long weeks, the largest, most drawn-out battle of the Second World War in western Europe. Battered and exhausted, the Allied forces fought not only the German troops, who were well-versed in winter warfare, but also the frigid, relentless winter conditions.

January 28, 1945, marked the official end of the Battle of the Bulge. There were more than 180,000 American and German casualties. Of these, 80,987 casualties were Americans, including 19,000 killed and 15,000 captured. Although the German troops had rallied once more to defend their homeland, the majority of the Third Reich's reserves of men and materiel were now used up. And the outcome of the battle had shown the world that the Allied forces could successfully check the advance of the German troops.

Less than one year after the Normandy landing, the war against Germany was at end. Hitler committed suicide on April 30. On May 8, 1945, the remaining German forces surrendered unconditionally. V-E (Victory in Europe) Day was met with cries of joy, even though it was feared that victory over Japan might take awhile longer.

Indeed, further bitter fighting with the Japanese continued in the Pacific theater. The Americans needed a strategy that would quickly turn the tables on the Japanese—and they soon found one.

When President Franklin D. Roosevelt died in April 1945, he was succeeded by Harry S. Truman. At about this time, physicists were completing a major, secret project on harnessing atomic power. This new power would take the form of a bomb with unprecedented destructive scope. News of the scientists' progress with the Manhattan Project reached President Truman in Potsdam, Germany, at a meeting of Allied leaders in mid-July 1945.

Based on what he learned of the Manhattan Project's success, Truman felt he had to issue an ultimatum to Japan demanding that they either surrender or face devastation by atomic weapons. The Japanese ignored the threat, and on August 6, 1945, the Enola Gay, an American B-29 aircraft, dropped an atomic bomb over the Japanese industrial center at Hiroshima.

Despite mass destruction and loss of civilian lives, the Japanese remained silent. On August 9, the United States dropped a second atomic weapon on the city of Nagasaki. Five days later, on August 14, the Japanese announced their decision to surrender. The articles of surrender were signed by Japanese government officials onboard the American battleship *Missouri* in Tokyo Bay on September 2, 1945.

At last, World War II had ended. The Allies had emerged victorious, and the United States had established for itself an unprecedented position of power, influence, and prestige.

But despite the best efforts of the VFW and all American citizens, the costs of World War II to America, and to the world, were beyond counting.

All told, 14 million men bearing arms lost their lives. Many more innocent civilians died in the crossfire and, of course, as a result of the grisly Holocaust. The United States counted 408,306 dead and another 670,846 wounded.

In carrying out their duties in the Pacific arena, American soldiers were tenacious, confident—even brash by many standards. But their confidence in America's armed might and the belief that the forces for right would eventually triumph held them in good stead through times of adversity, even when the challenges of combat were overwhelming.

The VFW and World War II

Just like its predecessor in 1914, World War II changed the world dramatically and for all time. The VFW played a significant role in making this change a positive one for the veterans of World War II who were able finally to return home. Here and elsewhere, the VFW's mobilization efforts during the war provided backbone for the campaign to make conditions better for returning veterans.

The VFW Service Officers School in Dearborn, Michigan, held intensive courses in how to handle Veterans Administration claims, adjudication work, and reemployment opportunities for veterans. Discharged and disabled World War II veterans formed the largest part of the corps of service officers recruited for this training program. Salaries were paid partially by VFW Departments and the National Headquarters.

The VFW also met with labor union officials to discuss ways in which returning veterans could be assisted in finding work. During this time, the VFW strongly advocated preferential treatment for veterans in employment, on-the-job training, seniority rights, and reemployment rights.

In 1944, the VFW was instrumental in getting the GI Bill of Rights, formally entitled the Servicemen's Readjustment Act of 1944, passed into law. Considered revolutionary at the time, it had far-reaching effects:

Some 7.8 million World War II veterans received college educations or vocational training compliments of the GI Bill. Two million more were able to get on-the-job training. A housing boom after World War II was the result of the 5,120,000 home loans granted to former service men and women. These loans totalled more than $43 billion (including loans for farms and businesses).

The GI Bill has been the basis for virtually all major veterans entitlements granted by Congress since 1944 for veterans of the Korean War, the Cold War, the Vietnam War, and, most recently, of Operation Desert Storm. It has more than paid for itself: You have only to consider that the better-educated, higher-salaried veterans who took advantage of their rights under the Bill now contribute nearly $1 billion a year in higher taxes.

The VFW laid the groundwork for the GI Bill with its 1943 call for a 10-point veterans program including the following items:

- Educational and training aid for veterans
- VA hospital care for those with at least 90 days service
- Continuation of military pay for six months after honorable discharge
- An escalator clause in compensation packages
- A requirement that three-tenths of a government contractor's employees be veterans
- An extra 20% in compensation, pension, and retired pay for disabled veterans with overseas service
- Veterans preference in all public employment
- Pensions for widows and orphans of deceased veterans
- Pensions for veterans unable to work, or who have a service-connected disability of ten percent or more
- VA jurisdiction over all veterans programs, and expansion of the VA and the Veterans Employment Service.

The VFW also successfully pressed for equalization of pay among all branches of the service and initiated the amendment to the National Service Life Insurance to provide $5,000 insurance for those killed between October 8, 1940, and April 19, 1942, before the National Service Life Insurance went into force.

Another VFW achievement involved giving free postage to service personnel during their term of service, along with increases in base pay from $21 to $30 a month (later increased to $50).

Also thanks to VFW support, allowances for spouses and dependent parents of service men and women were instituted. And the VFW fully supported Public Law 16, which established mandatory rehabilitation services for disabled veterans.

Other legislation which was also sponsored by VFW provided for home care and burial for World War II veterans on the same basis as World War I veterans; permanent retention of a veteran on the pension rolls if he or she had been listed for 10 years or was age 65; mustering out pay with a larger amount for overseas veterans and additional pay ($10 per month) for combat infantrymen; and, finally, the awarding of a Combat Infantry Badge.

The fighting men and uniformed women of World War II endured extreme hardship. They endured filth, heat, freezing cold, insect bites, numerous diseases, and constant movement with nowhere to rest their tired feet or bodies. They persevered against tremendous odds—and succeeded. They fought with a belief in democracy and freedom lodged firmly in their hearts. They fought for their buddies, their families, and our great nation.

America's World War II heroes also saved the world from what could have been a horrible fate indeed. They didn't do it to become heroes, but just because it had to be done.

As we now mark the 50-year anniversary of this momentous conflict, we should pause and remember the soldiers, sailors, leaders, "Rosie Riveters," and all the ordinary people who lived through these extraordinary times, and gave up so much in order that the world might remain free. They stood up to the forces of evil and made sure our world changed for the better. They rescued human dignity and united the spirit of our great nation, paving the way for prosperity and liberty for generations to come.

VI

KOREA, THE FORGOTTEN WAR

When the 90,000-strong, Russian-trained North
Korean Army swarmed across the 38th Parallel on the
Korean peninsula, invading South Korea on June 25,
1950, Americans were not anxious to fight another war.
Nor was our nation prepared to stage another major
military effort. World War II had ended only five years
before. Some questioned whether war in Korea might
be a wasted effort. While the Korean War proved to be
a decisive conflict waged against communism, it is also
one of the least remembered wars of the 20th century.

After America welcomed its troops home and celebrated victory over Germany and Japan, the public
interest turned to national, rather than international
affairs. The federal government was working to maintain a balanced budget and to reduce the national debt
without raising taxes. The military budget had been cut
by one-third. Troop levels had been reduced from six
million strong in World War II to only 590,000 by the
beginning of the Korean War. Many well-trained,
superbly equipped divisions were disbanded for lack of
need. Therefore, when war broke out in Korea in 1950,
the Armed Forces were skeletons of their former selves.

Politically, though, American involvement in Korea
was an imperative. President Harry Truman had laid
down a specific foreign policy in his containment
doctrine, inaugurated in 1947 to hold the line against
communism. The Containment Doctrine included a
radically new policy designed for the Cold War, namely,
"foreign aid" provided for war-torn countries so that
they might rebuild their societies and economies and
thereby provide their own defense against the encroach-
ments of communism. And "foreign aid" could mean

a lot more than just a monetary hand-out, particularly where communist aggression had to be met and checked.

So, immediately after July 25, a mad scramble got under way in the United States to mobilize the military forces, organize and distribute the troops, and marshal the necessary equipment for waging battle.

Because of the sensitive nature of the war and its potential for far-reaching consequences, American forces stationed in Europe also had to be reinforced, in order to offset the Soviet Union's uncompromising position and heavy involvement in Korea.

Back home, the General Reserve was strengthened, in part so that trained men and non-commissioned officers could be taken from home-based regular Army units and sent to the Far East. Unassigned, individual reservists were called to fill in the holes left in the regular army units and to flesh out both the Korea-bound units and the National Guard. In this emergency situation, all existing enlistments in the Army were extended for 12 months.

Many who had fought in World War II were pressed back into service, and they soon found themselves on troop ships bound for Korea. Some hadn't fired a gun since World War II. Approximately 20% of the soldiers who served in the Korean War were drawn from the pool of World War II veterans.

In addition, a draft was instituted, even though only about 1,700,000 of the 8,000,000 draft-age young men were called to serve. Inequities in the Selective Service system allowed over-lenient deferment provisions, influenced as well by the fact that this was considered to be only a limited conflict. Men between 18 and 25 were encouraged to volunteer to be inducted and serve for a period of 24 months.

Korea was America's first modern "limited war," limited by the scope and geography of the conflict. The

Pentagon's military plans didn't include provisions for such a limited war—only a worldwide conflict. This caused confusion and additional problems for government and military strategists. Each day, new plans were drawn up and altered to meet the new conditions of a new crisis. Direction from the top was not as smooth or efficient as it had been in the final days of World War II.

As with anything "new," the public and news media followed events closely during the first year of the war. Afterwards, however, as the truce talks began and the conflicts became more limited, public interest in what was happening in Korea quickly faded.

In 1952, a GI wrote: "the men in Korea were the forgotten men; the U.S. was aware of the conflict in Korea only in the sense that taxes were higher. The soldiers in Korea envied those at home living in a nation mentally at peace while physically at war." Despite the American GIs' awareness that they were not being held in the hearts and minds of Americans back home, one European observer commented that these GIs displayed an "amazing ability to endure adversity with grace."

And Army historian Brigadier General S.L.A. Marshall called the men of the Eighth Army "the hardest-hitting, most workman-like soldiers I have yet seen in our uniforms in the course of three wars."

Despite this praise, there was no mass mobilization at home like that of World War II. Many Americans showed little interest in a war taking place halfway around the world in a country they couldn't even find on a map. Only about 30% to 35% of the American people favored the war, according to Gallup Polls taken at the time. And many politicians were less than enthusiastic about it.

In other words, the Korean War seemed to affect only those who served and their loved ones left behind. Others either tried or tended to "forget" what was going on, the sacrifices that were being made on their behalf.

While back home most Americans were enjoying a general prosperity, GIs fought and lost their lives in Korea.

American soldiers sent to Korea found themselves exposed to extremely inhospitable climatic and geographic conditions. The Korean hillsides were steep, and the rainy season was so hot and steamy that perspiration caused soldiers' clothes to rot. Often, rice paddies gave off a nauseating stench of human feces, used as a fertilizer.

In the words of author Robert Leckie, winter in Korea descended like "a cold, howling, white beast—wet, raw and devouring." The temperature in the day might rise to zero or 20 degrees. By nightfall, it dropped to 20 or 30 degrees below zero.

Everything froze—weapons, food, even human flesh. Pancakes froze before they could be eaten and hot coffee was cold before the soldier could get it to his lips. Weapons refused to fire, misfired, or just broke completely. Grenades wouldn't explode. Water-cooled machine guns were filled with antifreeze to keep them operating correctly.

Frostbite stiffened fingers. Foxholes couldn't be dug because the ground was frozen rock-solid. Cover usually had to be found behind rocks or in crevices. At times, the frozen bodies of dead enemy soldiers were stacked for protection or cover.

Clothes had to be layered to keep the soldiers even moderately warm. Rubberized boots caused feet to sweat and then resulted in frostbite, claiming toes or whole feet. Caution had to be exercised not to warm hands too quickly by a fire, since the pain could prove excruciating. You also had to be careful not to sweat too much, because otherwise you might freeze to death in your own perspiration.

Blood for operations and transfusions could freeze as well, so plasma was of no use in some areas. If a wounded soldier was left too long with an open cut or torn, bloody flesh, gangrene quickly set in and all hope was lost. Medical corpsmen walked the battlelines to distribute morphine injections; before they could administer the shots, they had to stuff the syringe tubes in their mouths to thaw out the liquid inside.

To keep up morale in these horrible conditions, American military leaders devised a troop rotation system. But rotation offered mixed blessings: On the one hand, the spirit of the troops was uplifted; on the other, the efficiency of the fighting units was believed to be impaired. "Rest and Recuperation" (R&R) was another technique used to alleviate the tension of the limited warfare.

But the American GIs, who fought this war of containment under conditions of extreme adversity, were a tenacious group of men. Many felt that their performance in combat was nothing short of miraculous.

The American force comprised a varied collection of soldiers old and new, who had been hurriedly assembled for the Korean conflict. Some had fought at Iwo Jima or Guadalcanal. Many others were bright-eyed teenagers or just past their teenage years—brave boys who were eager and willing to do their part, whatever it might be. The old and new merged in the crucible of Korea: fighting at Pusan, crossing the Naktong River, and climbing the wall at Inchon. By the time they reached Seoul, every soldier was well-seasoned and battle-trained.

The offensive part of the war for the American soldier occurred during the first year, from June 1950 through June 1951, at which time truce talks began by common consent. For the next two years, most of the action took place in a "wait-and-see" position near the 38th parallel, involving duels with artillery fire and periodic struggles among the infantry. Finally, a demarcation line was settled on in negotiations ending

November 27, 1951. This marked the end to all offensive action.

The war then turned into something resembling a patrol action, similar in its cadence to the trench warfare of World War I. Fighting took place mostly at night. Soldiers crept through the barbed wire and crawled through the mine fields, often laying in ambush for hours on end.

The Korean War contains some famous and memorable battles. There were the battles over the Pusan Perimeter, Inchon, and the Chosin Reservoir, but most of the others were lost in the unwritten pages of history. Much of the war was fought in less than conventional forms of warfare—in bloody raids, ambushes, on ridges and rocky hills, and in early morning attacks.

For the first time in any war in our history, the United States Air Force fought as a separate service in Korea. They were, of course, the main combatants in the aerial war, but they were also critical players in assisting with airlifts and in evacuating the wounded by air.

The first "jet-to-jet" combat occurred during the Korean War. The "boys in blue" flew 341,269 sorties and made 839 MiG-15 kills during the war. Air and naval forces were an extremely important part of the war—but as in all wars, the greatest burden of the fight was borne by the infantry.

America paid a heavy price for its noble crusade to contain communism and save South Korea. Over 90% of the non-Korean UN combat dead were Americans. The United States suffered 33,629 combat deaths; 103,284 GIs were wounded seriously enough to be hospitalized. The survival rate was greatly improved over that of World War II, however, because of the evacuation by aircraft.

Helicopters were used for the first time to airlift the wounded from the battlefields to Mobile Army Surgical Hospitals (MASH). Although 22% of those wounded in action died, only 2.5% died after reaching the hospital.

At least 7,140 prisoners of war (POWs) were taken. Thirty-eight percent of them (2,701) died in captivity because of the extremely inhumane conditions in the prison camps in North Korea. Today, there are still 8,194 American soldiers who are listed "missing in action" (MIA) or unidentified from the Korean War. Leaders of VFW continue to work on the POW/MIA issues, often traveling around the world to meet with the responsible parties and trying to obtain information and/or the release of surviving prisoners. The VFW also continues to urge our federal government to send delegations and arrange talks and information missions to make sure that these men are not forgotten and that everything possible is done to free the ones still alive.

The communist foes who wreaked havoc on South Korea were actually two distinct armies, representing two different countries: The North Korean People's Army (NKPA) and the Chinese Communist Forces (CCF).

The Chinese contributed dogged, determined soldiers to the war effort. Over 300,000 came across the Yalu River to fight on behalf of their comrades in North Korea. The Chinese soldiers were well-trained, with a tradition of victory acquired and honed during their internal revolutionary struggles. A large number were young peasants from North China, sturdy, strong, and stoic. Added to this group were the professionals who had served under the former Chinese war lords, Nationalists who had joined the communist military after the defeat of Chiang Kai-shek, and oldtimers who had fought the war lords, the Japanese, and Chiang Kai-shek and who now were fighting for Mao Tse-tung. These were one and all career soldiers: In the Chinese Communist Forces, retirement was allowed only by disability or death.

These seasoned soldiers could endure much hardship and live on few rations. To counter their lack of artillery, they attacked at night under the cloak of darkness. They would crawl toward the enemy's positions and, with a sudden blast of bugles, shrill whistles, and clanging cymbals, they would charge upon them, attempting to fight at close range with bayonets and grenades. Their leaders were some of the world's most experienced commanders; some had been leading troops since World War I; some had never been defeated.

General Sung Shine-lun, the Chinese leader renowned for his ruthless guerrilla warfare, bravery, and bad temper, circulated propagandistic pamphlets to inflame his troops. One of the pamphlets he used had been written by a Russian naval captain, describing the "barbarous" American Marines. Shine-lun would goad his troops with his own speech, as reported in Robert Leckie's book, *The March to Glory*:

"Soon we will meet the American Marines in battle. We will destroy them. . . . Kill these Marines as you would snakes in your homes."

When the armistice was signed, no cannons were fired or celebrations held in the streets of American cities and towns. The news of the war's end was accepted, not cheered. Americans were not accustomed to an inconclusive victory, so they didn't know how to react to a cease-fire and the dividing up of a conquered nation. In the end, Korean War veterans were just ignored and overlooked.

Few Americans realized the global significance of the confrontation or its outcome. In fact, the Korean War wasn't even designated a war until 1958. The government preferred to call it a "police action" or a "conflict."

Of course, to the men fighting on the fronts, the reality of 24,000 artillery shells a day landing on U.S. lines, the hot stench of the steamy rainy summers, and the frigid, icy winters could only spell war, in one of its most brutal manifestations.

James Brady, author of *The Coldest War,* who served as a rifle platoon leader in Korea, compared the war with the primitive fighting in Flanders Fields during World War I or "Grant's siege lines before Petersburg, Virginia, in the Civil War."

Former GI Robert Leckie remembers vividly a mass burial ceremony he attended during the Chosin Reservoir campaign. Two bulldozers stood ready by the hollow of a artillery excavation filled "with snow-covered, blanketed shapes." The chaplain's voice could be heard: "Remember, man, that dust thou art, and unto dust thou shalt return... out of dust shalt thou rise again." Then clods of frozen dirt could be heard as they were dropped by the bulldozers to cover the bodies. "The earth of Korea closed over these Americans," he has written.

To mark the grave, an artillery aiming stake was driven into the ground. Soldiers then filed back to their units, mourning friends and fellow Americans who had made the full, final sacrifice for their country. With heavy hearts, they returned to their duty posts, knowing full well that tomorrow would only bring more dead.

But, in some ways, this "forgotten" war goes on even today. Although the armistice was signed nearly 40 years ago, troops still remain in South Korea. And there is the unanswered question of the POWs and MIAs. Of the 8,000 Americans missing in action in Korea, 389 remain officially unaccounted for.

The VFW and the War America Forgot

As it had done for with other groups of veterans, the VFW worked to provide support and secure benefits for those who served in Korea when they returned home. But because of the specifically hostile environment in which these men and women served, many suffered severe shell shock and mental traumas. Medical evacuation by airlift depicted in the movie and television series, "M*A*S*H," allowed many lives to be saved that otherwise would have been lost, but many wounds and losses of limb required special, long-term treatment. VFW pushed to see that veterans suffering extreme injury received the proper medical care.

And, when the war was over, the VFW seized the occasion to work for the passage of the Veterans Readjustment Assistance Act, which became Public Law 550 in 1952, thus creating a new, updated GI Bill of Rights. VFW also tried to help integrate veterans of the Korean conflict back into mainstream society.

But the VFW is still fighting for thousands who never came home from Korea—the MIAs. VFW Resolution 420, Concerning the Korean War MIA Issue, calls for the Administration "to exert maximum economic and diplomatic pressure on North Korea" to resolve this vital matter.

VFW is also pushing for a national tribute to all who served in Korea, particularly those who died. It has made contributions totalling over $600,000 toward the construction of the planned Korean War memorial.

Although it has been a long time in coming, a national memorial *will* be built in Washington, D.C., scheduled for completion by mid-1993. Some 40,000 Americans gave their lives on behalf of freedom in Korea, and it is only fitting that those sacrifices be appropriately recognized and remembered.

It is never too late to honor America's heroes. And there is no better time than today for the American people to express their gratitude to the 1.5 million GIs who served in Korea during those dangerous years.

Perhaps now America can come to grips with the war's outcome. As historian Richard Rovere wrote, "We accomplished in Korea whàt we set out to do—repel armed aggression and demonstrate the efficacy of collective security. . . . History will cite it as the turning point of the world struggle against communism."

Distinguished author and decorated Korean War veteran Harry G. Summers provides a fitting summation of the significance of Korea in world history:

"Korean veterans, take heart. Your real memorial was the collapse of the Berlin Wall and the disintegration of world communism, events that you set in motion by your defense of freedom so many years ago."

At last, the brave warriors of the "forgotten war" will be remembered the way they should be.

VII

VIETNAM: A NATION DIVIDED

The Vietnam War, like the American Civil War, pulled our nation apart at the seams. But the Vietnam War is in a class by itself in one way: No other war in our history has been so misunderstood by our citizens, who were too removed from the causes and the battleground to have a clear picture of this conflict. While the war was being carried out in faraway Asia, the scene at home was often just as chaotic. It was common to see protestors filling the streets, shouting their disapproval of "an unjust war." And the protests didn't end there, either.

As more and more young men were drafted by the Selective Service System, the System itself became the target of the protest. Draft cards were burned in public, sit-ins were held in front of recruitment offices, and pickets at local draft boards increased. Congress swiftly responded by making penalties tougher for violation of the draft laws: Fines up to $10,000 were levied and prison sentences could go up to five years.

After American combat troops entered Vietnam in March 1965, the draft resistance movement grew, and anti-war demonstrations became larger, more violent, and more frequent. The conflict in many Americans' minds was played out on the streets, as the protestors' signs of "We won't go!" were met by counter-demonstrators shouting, "USA, Love it or Leave it!"

But what was happening on the streets did not necessarily reflect the feelings of the largest segment of the population. In the early years of the war, the majority of American people wholeheartedly supported America's efforts in Vietnam. They fully agreed with the government's contention that the war was necessary to contain international communism, and they endorsed government's confident assumption that the war would eventually be won.

However, as the nation's commitment to the conflict grew, contradictions in policy and purpose began to arise. Disagreements appeared over the way the war should be fought. Some favored an all-out commitment to provide all the war materiel necessary to win the war promptly, while others believed that military action should be continued at a steady pace, taking a back seat to possible peace negotiations.

Meanwhile, the anti-war sentiment turned on the service members returning from their tours of duty in Vietnam. Flags were burned in the streets. Service members were openly spit on, reviled, and shunned. In a bizarre, utterly unfair twist of fate, the soldiers themselves had become a symbol for a war many people had grown to hate. So they were hated—for having responded to their country's call to duty!

Young soldiers were shocked when they returned home from Vietnam to hear chants of "baby killer" and have people turn their backs on them. War veterans had not been treated this shabbily since the Spanish American War and Philippine Insurrection which parallelled this era, and sparked the establishment of the VFW.

One young man—we'll call him "Bill"—remembers how eagerly he anticipated his arrival back home in 1969. Only 19 years old when he had gone to serve in Vietnam the year before, Bill said he felt as if he were 50 when it was time to come home. Vietnam was, in his own words, "worse than any hell I could imagine!"

With 122 mm rockets streaking through the air, mortar shells exploding, booby traps planted everywhere he turned, and ambushes waiting at every corner, each day in Vietnam could have been Bill's last. The lulls in fighting could be just as bad, because the anticipation of what lay ahead was almost more than a human could bear. Bill saw men seriously injured and killed on the field of battle.

After all that he had seen and experienced first-hand, Bill was in a hurry to get home. But nothing could have prepared him for the homecoming he received.

Walking into the Los Angeles airport, still in his uniform, and planting his feet firmly on American soil once more, he was met by a crowd of strangers, who jeered at him and his comrades with insults of "murderer," "babykiller," and other unprintable terms of abuse. Then someone he didn't know came up to him and spat directly into his face! The shock was almost more than he could bear.

In his book, *Homecoming: When the Soldiers Returned from Vietnam,* reporter Bob Greene talks about the "emotional shutdown" many Vietnam veterans experienced. Naturally, they weren't prepared for the cruel treatment they received in public and in private, sometimes at the hands of friends and loved ones they thought would be happy to welcome them home. Simply in order to cope with their hurt and disappointment, many of these young men built impenetrable, dangerous psychological walls around themselves.

Thousands of returning soldiers experienced severe, recurring nightmares, as they were forced to recall the horrors of war in Vietnam. Treatment to settle their troubled unconscious minds was often difficult, drawn-out, and extremely painful for these war-shocked veterans. In some cases, the nightmares included details of the treatment they received on their return home.

Another soldier, known as John, returned from Vietnam minus his left arm. In many ways, John felt blessed to have gotten out of the war alive, so he had little difficulty adjusting to a new life with only one arm. The people around him, however, had a harder time. He was often stopped and asked where and how he had lost his arm. When he told them it had happened in Vietnam, he sometimes got answers like, "Well, then, you deserve it," or "It serves you right."

Countless cases of abuse, insults, and avoidance have been chronicled by soldiers returning from this unpopular war. Many Vietnam veterans were refused drinks in bars or service in restaurants. Others found that their tour of duty made employers hesitant about giving them a job. Strangers often refused to sit by them in public places if they had their uniforms on.

Rather than a red carpet rolled out for them, soldiers had eggs and trash thrown at them as they disembarked from the planes in their home towns. Many of these servicemen and women weren't expecting homecoming parades or a hero's welcome; however, they felt they at least deserved respect for having served their country.

A common thread runs through the thoughts of many who served during the war years in Vietnam: Despite what anyone might feel about the causes, purpose, or outcome of the war, these brave men and women knew that they had gone and done the job their country asked them to do. They had served their country honorably and, now that they were home, they just wanted to live normal lives and hold onto their sanity.

Unfortunately, many Americans would make it difficult for them to hold onto these simple beliefs—or to let them feel as though they could become part of the fabric of American life again.

One Vietnam veteran summed up the feelings of many in his letter, reprinted in Bob Greene's *Homecoming:* "A Vietnam vet could take being spat on by one person. What broke our hearts was being spat on by our country."

Their reaction was particularly tragic considering how devastating combat in itself was for Vietnam veterans. The letters home from Vietnam were truly heart-breaking in their expressions of bewilderment, pain, and personal anguish. As in any war, the bulk of the fighting was placed on young men, no older than 18, 19, or 20. Writing home to his mother, one young GI expressed himself in these words: "I can't tell you the horrible things I've seen. I may be the same outside but I can't ever be the same inside. War forces a boy to be a man. The fear is something I can't describe. Nobody can watch a man die and stay the same. I'm doing the best I can. I want you to be proud of me. Right now, I'm just thankful to be alive. I love you."

Every war brings sacrifice, death, and physical and emotional suffering. However, when emotional support and understanding is absent at home the scars of war are increased. It has taken years for that emotional toll just to be recognized, much less dealt with!

The horrors of war, which turn boys and girls into adults, were compounded in Vietnam by the shabby treatment GIs received at home and the guilt they were made to feel by a large segment of the American public. With this war, a tragic episode in our history remains one of our country's political and military controversies, our soldiers got caught in the middle and were the ones who truly suffered the "slings and arrows of outrageous fortune."

Fortunately for these deserving men and women, there was one refuge where people would understand and care for these veterans' pressing needs—the Veterans of Foreign Wars. VFW volunteers visited troops in the field and were instrumental in efforts to counteract anti-war demonstrations at home. The VFW offered a wide range of support services to returning veterans. They worked to make sure that these veterans were not left out in the cold, without the assistance they deserved and so desperately needed in order to rebuild their lives.

On the national level, the VFW campaigned hard for a Vietnam-era GI Bill, which became law in 1967. Likewise, a top priority then and now was the resolution and concern for the fate of the POWs and MIAs.

With the advent of better, highly sophisticated medical technology and more efficient emergency evacuation by helicopter of the severely wounded, more lives were saved in Vietnam than in previous wars. The percentage of wounded soldiers who survived to total combat casualties for the U.S. Army in Vietnam was 81.3%. In other words, for every 10 soldiers wounded, eight survived. For World War II, this ratio was only 70.7%; in the Korean War, it had climbed slightly to 73.7%.

Even though the rate of fatalities was down, incidences of paraplegia and of multiple amputations increased dramatically during the Vietnam War. Booby traps, mortar shells, mines, and explosives caused many to be severely disabled. Of the 153,303 wounded who required hospitalization, approximately half of these were permanently disabled.

Because there was an unprecedented need for prosthetics, the VFW made a strong case to the VA to ensure that artificial limbs and devices needed by veterans were properly fitted. The Prosthetic and Sensory Aids Service (PSAS) of the VA was dissolved in 1973, and the clinical programs were transferred to the Surgical Service. This meant that, during the 1970s, disabled veterans were forced to fight for state-of-the-art prosthetic devices. In 1977, PSAS was reactivated by the VA at the insistence of veterans organizations such as the VFW.

Working with the VA, the VFW helped Vietnam veterans to file claims, receive help at counseling centers, and receive benefits to compensate for exposure to Agent Orange, radiation, post-traumatic stress disorders (PTSD), and other problems caused by the effects of war.

The years during and following the Vietnam War were challenging times for the institutions and the people of this great democratic nation, all of whom were divided within and among themselves about the meaning of this conflict. Some felt that the only way to heal the rifts and bitterness was to create a memorial.

After years of struggling to raise the funds, get the approvals, and garner a consensus on the design and location of this monument, a group of dedicated Americans built the Vietnam Veterans Memorial in Washington, D.C., centrally located on the Mall between the Lincoln Memorial and the Washington Monument. VFW members alone contributed over $200,000 to this important testament to the sacrifices of thousands of brave men and women. The Memorial was dedicated in 1982, some nine years after the end of the war.

The Wall, as it is called, contains the names of the 58,183 Americans who lost their lives in this "thankless war." Their names are engraved, one after another, on two black stone walls, each of which extends some 246 feet along the Mall.

This Wall is a source of healing for many veterans whose comrades were killed in the war and for families who lost a son, husband, or father in Vietnam. I'll let the people who visited the Wall tell you in their own words about the pain they were able to release at this special memorial:

One cool, gray day, William W. Pollack, a retired disabled veteran, decided to pay a visit to the Memorial before he moved away from the Washington area. More than two decades ago, he had fought in Vietnam and "lost a part of myself in that distant and devastated land." The biting wind on the Mall made him wince from the arthritis that had set in his old wounds. But as he approached the Wall and surveyed the names there, he began to pray for those who had suffered and given so much and for their families. Tears were released that he had kept firmly inside for more than 20 years.

Walking alongside the Monument, he felt a spirit of "true serenity." By the time he found the name of an old friend, the day had grown even colder. Touching it, though, Pollack felt the stone was "warm and vibrant; creating a feeling I shall carry with me wherever I go."

So, without knowing the outcome of his visit, Pollack had taken a giant step forward in healing his own soul. His brief time spent at the Memorial helped him overcome the hate, the waste, and the anger of many years gone by.

Another Vietnam veteran, Lewis Puller, Jr., vividly recalls the 1982 Dedication Ceremony of the Vietnam Memorial in his book, *Fortunate Son.* He remembers the large crowd that was present, perhaps around 150,000 people. He felt unaccustomed to being in such a crowd—especially one that was so incredibly orderly.

Having lost both legs and portions of his hands in the war, Puller advanced through the crowd in his wheelchair, heading for the area reserved for people in wheelchairs. As he went by, hands kept reaching out to touch his arms and shoulders. He heard voices and echoes of "Welcome home, brother." He was so moved by the warm reception that he wanted to run back and forth along the Wall calling out the names of each soldier who had died—so that all the world might hear.

On his first return visit to the Memorial, which was to become an "often repeated rite of homage," Puller brought a single red rose to pin next to his friend's name. Seeing his own reflection in the polished stone, Puller understood "how inextricably linked the memorial and I were by the bloodshed of my brothers." He felt the Memorial was "in the end, comforting, spiritual, rooted in the present, but, like me, looking backward in sorrow and anger and forward in hope and exultation."

You can visit the Vietnam Veterans Memorial in the bright sunshine of the morning or in the darkness of night and almost always find hundreds of onlookers—friends, families, wellwishers, or just curious tourists—making their pilgrimage to its beautiful Wall nestled in a wooded grove. The Vietnam Veterans Memorial is visited by more people than any other site in the nation's capital. Of those who come, some are young, some are quite old, but all are reverent and speak in the hushed tones of respect; respect that was significantly absent during the conflict itself.

People routinely leave offerings on the pathway leading visitors along the Wall. American flags, unit patches, military clothing, photographs, letters, fresh flowers—thousands of small tributes of personal remembrance are strewn at the foot of this long granite wall that means so much to so many.

More than 2.6 million Americans served in Vietnam. Of these, 303,704 were wounded (half were hospitalized); 75,000 were permanently disabled; 58,156 were killed; and 2,348 Americans remain unaccounted for.

Approximately 7,484 American women served in the Vietnam War, too. Of these, 85% were nurses. Eight women were killed in the line of duty, and their names are inscribed on the Wall along with their fallen comrades. VFW has currently joined the effort to raise funds for the Vietnam Women's Memorial project, which plans to erect a separate statue honoring these women near the Vietnam Veterans Memorial in the nation's capital.

Vietnam was a symbol of our nation divided. The VFW hopes that Americans never forget the pain and suffering of those who served so valiantly to preserve world freedom. All caring Americans also hope never again to witness a country torn asunder during such a difficult time.

VIII

THE ERA OF VIOLENT PEACE: THE COLD WAR

Less than one year after the end of World War II, as a result of jockeying for power by the Soviet Union in the Middle East and the eastern portions of the European continent, an Iron Curtain descended, dividing east and the west in an uneasy truce. With a few bold strokes, Joseph Stalin shattered the former Allies' hope for lasting world peace and true democracy. Within a short time after the war, an uncrossable line was drawn between the democracies of the west and the communist countries of the east.

Even though the defeat of Nazi Germany had freed the world from one evil tyrant, and although the Allied forces had emerged victorious in the hard-fought battle, the peace following World War II would only be brief, and yet another dictator would threaten the world once more.

Throughout the war years, the Grand Alliance of the United States, Great Britain, and the Soviet Union had been shaky at best, alternating between warm amicability and tense caution. Although the wartime experience had gone some way toward alleviating the mistrust between Americans and Soviets, the gulf between the two nations was still wide. Now, deep-seated suspicions and fundamental differences flared up over the ways these two great powers envisioned the shape of the post-war world.

Although the United States, Great Britain, and the Soviet Union were able to reach agreement on a number of issues—notably the establishment of the United Nations—the atmosphere remained strained between the two superpowers of the West and the totalitarian regime of the East.

The first shots of the Cold War were fired in 1945 near Trieste, Italy, at the border with Yugoslavia, on the Adriatic Sea. The guns of World War II had barely ceased firing when U.S. troops were dispatched to prevent the spread of communism in a new kind of war of containment, two years before the Cold War was officially declared by President Harry Truman in 1947. A new era of violent peace was ushered in, one which would require U.S. troops to be sent to foreign shores in different parts of the world periodically over the next 45 years.

So, rather than enjoying a post-war free world, which is what many Americans had envisioned, the United States was forced to lead the western world in countering the threat of Communism and containing further expansion of the Soviet Union.

One crisis after another arose in the ensuing years. First, Stalin refused to pull his occupation forces out of Iran in March 1946. In response, the United States fired off a threatening ultimatum to the Soviet Union. Stalin relented and withdrew his forces, but this was only his opening shot. Potential clashes in Turkey and Greece, where communist forces threatened to topple pro-Western governments, soon followed. With events such as these, it quickly became clear to the United States that the Soviet Union had begun instituting an aggressive foreign policy with only one possible goal in mind: world conquest.

On March 12, 1947, President Harry Truman appeared before the U.S. Congress and announced his intent to establish a policy of containment of communism, known as the Truman Doctrine. This doctrine formed the cornerstone of American foreign policy for more than twenty years; it had an impact long after it was officially abandoned in favor of a more conciliatory policy in the 1970s and 1980s.

The Truman Doctrine proclaimed that communism

was an ideological threat to world peace and a real threat to the stability of democratic governments throughout the world. Therefore, it became the policy of the United States government to assist pro-democratic forces anywhere in the world in their struggles against communism. The argument was put forth that, if one nation fell to communism, it could easily result in a "domino effect," causing the surrounding nations to topple as well.

Another building block of the containment doctrine involved the economic reconstruction of Western Europe, carried out in the name of the "Marshall Plan." By actively helping to rebuild a free Western Europe which could defend itself, the Americans tried to help create a strong deterrent to the spread of communism.

One of the first tests of this new world order came in the struggle over what to do with the vanquished Germany. The U.S., Great Britain, and France agreed to merge the three western zones of occupation (including the American, British, and French occupied sectors of Berlin) into a new West German republic.

The Soviet Union quickly responded with a blockade of the city of Berlin. Stalin wanted the country's western government to abandon its post in Berlin if Germany was to be officially divided. The Soviet occupation of Berlin lasted some ten months; U.S. troops retaliated by operating an airlift which brought food and supplies to the people in the city of Berlin. Stalin was finally forced to abandon the occupation, since the airlift had been so successful, keeping alive a city of 2,000,000 people and transforming it into a symbol of the West's commitment to resist the expansion of communism. Then, in October 1949, Germany was officially divided into two nations, the Federal Republic in the West and the Democratic Republic in the East.

The Berlin crisis catapulted the United States and the countries of Western Europe into a defensive alliance, formally called the North Atlantic Treaty Organization (NATO). The NATO agreement declared that an armed attack against one member country would be considered an attack against all NATO member countries, meaning that all might come to the immediate defense of their ally.

The Soviet Union countered by forming an alliance with the communist governments in Eastern Europe, which was later called the Warsaw Pact. In essence, though, the Warsaw Pact nations consisted of the countries which the Soviet Union had occupied during the Second World War, and to a large extent continued to occupy afterwards as well. Stalin took it as a *fait accompli* that his sphere of influence extended over Latvia, Lithuania, Estonia, Poland, Czechoslovakia, Hungary, Rumania, East Germany, and Bulgaria, since Soviet troops were already stationed there!

American influence in Western Europe was significantly enhanced by the NATO alliance. Soon, the United States became the major supplier to the NATO military forces, and General Dwight D. Eisenhower was named Supreme Commander of the Allied forces in Europe. By emerging as one of the world's two greatest powers, the United States soon witnessed an unprecedented expansion of its military's role in the world and a multiplying of its responsibilities around the globe.

In the decades that followed, Americans would once again send their young adults to fight in difficult, protracted wars, now in such remote corners of the globe as Korea and Vietnam. In the years between and after these conflicts, Americans would also send their sons and daughters to points scattered all over the world, where they were called to fight communist guerrilla forces in smaller, less publicized, yet equally dangerous conflicts. The Cold War would demand its share of America's fighting men just the same as any war.

Many Americans do not realize that our servicemen

and women made the same commitments and sacrifices in the Cold War and operations to preserve freedom, as were made in our country's declared wars. The fact is that many soldiers offered up the ultimate sacrifice—their lives. Thousands of others were wounded, lost limbs, and had their lives forever altered, every bit as much as the veterans who fought in World Wars I and II, Korea, and Vietnam.

The VFW knew all along that the Cold War was a "real" war for those who served in our nation's military. Therefore, the VFW took up the fight to ensure these veterans also received adequate medical treatment, respect, and the pensions and benefits they deserved.

One way America has shown its gratitude to those service members who served in the Cold War and other conflicts is with the award of an Armed Forces Expeditionary Medal (AFEM). Soldiers who served in any one of 20 separate military actions between 1958 and the recent "Operation Just Cause" in Panama in 1989 are eligible for this medal. It was specifically approved for operations where no other campaign medal existed.

One of these missions was "Operation Bluebat," a peacekeeping mission of the American military, deployed from July 1 to November 1, 1958, in defense of the shaky government then in control in Lebanon. Arab nationalists were threatening a violent overthrow of the Lebanese government, so President Eisenhower ordered 5,000 American Marines to land on the Lebanese beaches in mid-July. At the Operation's peak, there were about 14,500 Marine, Army, and Air Force troops stationed in Lebanon.

The United States answered the call of the Lebanese government for help under the Eisenhower Doctrine, which authorized the use of U.S. armed force in the Middle East at the request of a nation threatened by outside aggression. In this case, American troops were able to restore order at least temporarily. And casualties were slight: Only one soldier was killed, and one wounded.

From 1958 through 1964, an estimated 50,000 service members were also stationed in Vietnam. They were there to advise and assist the South Vietnamese armed forces in their fight against the communist aggressors, the Viet Cong, from the northern part of the country. During these early years, 250 Americans were killed in action, approximately 1,600 were wounded, and 11 Americans were listed as missing in action. One hundred seven deaths were attributable to non-hostile causes.

President Eisenhower stated that American support of the South Vietnamese government would help to preserve a "free" Vietnam. In doing so, he made a key reference to the "domino theory." He and many other government leaders were certain that if Vietnam fell to communism, the other small nations of Southeast Asia would inevitably follow. But throughout this period, although Eisenhower sent many troops to help in an advisory capacity, he continually refused to commit to a direct American military intervention in Vietnam.

Quemoy and Matsu, two islands off the coast of mainland China, became the scene of a show of force and escort operations by the Americans during the period August 23, 1958–June 1, 1963. Some 30,000 American military personnel were deployed in the waters surrounding these islands, in accordance with America's formal commitment to defend Formosa (now called Taiwan) and the Pescadores from armed attack by Communist China. U.S. troops repeatedly escorted Nationalist transports to a three-mile territorial limit off the islands. The purpose of this escort was to break the blockade imposed by Communist China and stop the bombardment of Nationalist boats. The American strategy was a success, and, fortunately, no American lives were lost in this operation.

Between August 1958 and January 1959, the United States deployed a military task force in the Taiwan

Straits to deter aggression against Nationalist China. Some 30,000 troops were sent to prevent the communist invasion of the island of Taiwan. Once again, the Americans were able to execute their strategy without incurring any casualties.

On another turbulent continent, Africa, "Operation New Tape," a United Nations peace-keeping mission (including a strong U.S. presence) was carried out to restore order during the civil war in the Belgian Congo (now Zaire) from July 14, 1960 to September 1, 1962. United Nations troops, equipment, and supplies were airlifted, and three eight-man crews of C-130 transports were deployed to the Congo to help oppose the bloodthirsty Congolese rebels. Injuries were sustained by U.S. troops, but no one was killed. A precarious order was restored, with U.N. troops continually ferrying around the Congo region.

Perhaps the most visible symbol of communism was the Berlin Wall, erected in 1961. Although no fighting occurred, tensions were so great that many feared the United States and the Soviet Union were on the brink of starting World War III. World attention was riveted to Berlin as the Soviets built the wall and President John F. Kennedy called up reservists "to prevent a war, not to fight a war."

In his typical belligerent, outspoken fashion, Soviet Premier Nikita Khrushchev said, "When I want the West to scream, I squeeze on Berlin." The United States responded to what amounted to a Soviet challenge by sending 1,500 men of the First Battle Group, 8th Infantry Division, from the U.S. Army base at Mannheim, West Germany to Berlin. They marched in six columns of 150 men each with 40 vehicles, at one point crossing through communist East Germany. Addressing them on their arrival in Berlin, Vice President Lyndon Johnson pledged that "all the resources of the mightiest nation in the world stand behind you."

The American show of military might was bolstered as U.S. High Command placed American air and ground forces in Europe on alert and conducted the largest maneuvers since World War II. Back in the States, 155,000 reservists and Guardsmen were called up, and Air National Guard units were mobilized. Other Naval, Army, and Air Force units were also placed on alert.

No shooting occurred, but the temperature of the stalemate ran continually high. On October 27, 1961, a confrontation between U.S. and Soviet troops across a 100-yard divide at "Checkpoint Charlie" provided one of the most potentially dangerous moments of the Cold War. Troops were on edge, almost straining at the bit to prove their mettle. The slightest sign of untoward aggression could have precipitated a major conflagration. Eventually, the Soviets backed down, but this incident permanently engraved the image of a world on the brink of war in the hearts of troops and peace-loving civilians around the world. War would be an ever-present possibility, particularly for the United States and the Soviet Union, every moment of every day throughout the 1960s, 1970s, and 1980s.

Those soldiers entrusted with guarding the Berlin Wall saw first-hand the horrors of communism. One soldier stationed there remembers a young man being riddled with bullets as he tried to escape from East Berlin to freedom. He was left to bleed to death in the middle of the "no man's land" between the two Berlins. His body would offer a visible deterrent to others who might contemplate an escape.

But it didn't stop many desperate souls from trying to beat the odds and make their way to a new life in a free world. Many of these civilians were blown up in mine fields or killed in a hail of rounds of automatic fire. Fierce Alsatian attack dogs were used to patrol the 200-yard strip of death by the Wall. More than 5,000 mercury vapor lights illuminated the area at night, making escapees an easy target for sharpshooting soldiers on watch. In spite of these risks, many individuals' desire for freedom was too strong to be allayed by the sight of gruesome deaths suffered by their comrades.

A tour of duty at the Berlin Wall left American service members with a vivid image of the horrors of life under communism. No second-hand experience could bring home the reality of the hopelessness and desperation of citizens living under repressive communist regimes in eastern Europe.

Gradually, the tensions across the barrier of the Berlin Wall lessened and the feverish pace of attempted escapes slowed. Occupation forces continued to serve there, maintaining a watch for freedom, but there were progressively fewer incidents.

But just because things had quieted down at the Berlin Wall, it didn't mean that the Cold War was over. The next crisis proved extremely provocative and potentially explosive. In part, this was because it took place practically in America's backyard.

Communism posed its most direct threat to the Western Hemisphere in the early 1960s, as the Soviet Union began to ship arms and missiles to its ally in the Caribbean, Cuba. American officials perceived that Khrushchev was planning to use Cuba as a launching pad to direct short-range nuclear missiles at the United States.

On April 17, 1961, approximately 1,300 members of an anticommunist Cuban exile force landed at Cuba's Bay of Pigs with the reluctant approval of President John F. Kennedy. This military brigade had been assembled in 1960 under the direction of President Dwight Eisenhower; it was armed and trained in Guatemala by the Central Intelligence Agency (CIA). Air cover was not provided for this operation, because of the fear that it might be viewed as "a full-fledged invasion."

It was doomed to failure. Cuban Premier Fidel Castro's troops routed the invading brigade in only two days. The Bay of Pigs had been a military and logistical fiasco, leaving egg on the face of American military leaders.

Just prior to the Bay of Pigs, several other "actions" took place in remote areas of the globe. An American counterinsurgency force was sent to Laos, which was on the verge of a Communist takeover, foreshadowing a similar chain of events and American involvement in Vietnam. In the Laotian episode, three American servicemen were killed in action, and several others were wounded.

"Operation Dragon Red" and "Operation Black," evacuation missions in the Congo, resulted in the rescue of some 2,000 Europeans and Americans.

As these confrontations continued to flare up in countries around the globe, the Cold War only got more bitter, with the opposing parties more determined to increase their influence in the world and the stakes even higher. Technologically, the race to be first or strongest consumed the energies of the two superpowers. Hopes were dimmed for any kind of nuclear disarmament when the Soviets vetoed a United Nations proposal for inspection of nuclear arms. And, on April 12, 1961, the U.S.S.R. sent the first man to orbit in space.

Events in Cuba didn't end with the Bay of Pigs invasion; indeed, they only got worse. The escalation of arms and missile shipments by the Soviets to Cuba eventually led to the most frightening show-down of all, what is today known as "the Cuban missile crisis," which took place in October 1962. President Kennedy threatened retaliation if the Soviet missiles were not taken off the Cuban island immediately. The Soviets didn't respond. For one full week, the world was perched fearfully on the brink of nuclear war.

As it is reported in the book, *Life in Camelot: The Kennedy Years* (Kunhardt & Kappler, eds.), President Kennedy stood firm but expressed the fear of many when he said:

"Today, every inhabitant of this planet must contemplate the day when it may no longer be habitable. Every man, woman, and child lives under a nuclear Sword of Damocles, hanging by the slenderest of threads, capable of being cut at any moment . . . by accident, miscalculation or madness. The weapons of war must be abolished before they abolish us."

In another operation to prevent the spread of Castro's influence in the Caribbean, the Dominican Republic became the scene of sporadic military action between April 28, 1965, and September 21, 1966. At the height of this crisis, 22,200 troops were sent ashore and 11,500 were stationed offshore.

And, of course, a strong American military presence in Korea was mandated by the terms of the Korean peace treaty. The United States committed approximately 320,000 troops to South Korea as a bulwark against communist North Korea and China between October 1, 1966, and June 30, 1974. While stationed along the border to deter North Korean aggression and combat possible infiltration, approximately 89 Americans were killed and 131 wounded in the line of duty. Although only a small percentage faced hostile fire in the demilitarized zone, or DMZ, the troops were on constant alert, never knowing when they could be fired on or when actual war might break out.

In Cambodia, U.S. troops, on two occasions in 1975, were called upon to evacuate or protect U.S. citizens. Marines engaged in ground fighting during the Mayaguez operation. Eighteen Marines were killed and 50 others were wounded in action.

With the end of the Vietnam War drawing near, the evacuation of Saigon, called "Operation Frequent

Wind," took place on April 29-30, 1975. A force of Marines came to help evacuate almost 7,000 people. During the operation, two Marine pilots lost their lives when their helicopters crashed in the sea.

Once again, events in the Middle East necessitated an American military presence. A peace-keeping force was sent to preserve relative stability in Lebanon from 1982 to 1984. At its peak, the deployment included 2,000 Marines. Here, casualties were much greater: 266 killed in action and 169 wounded.

The 1983 invasion of Grenada by forces of the United States involved 20,000 personnel. The purpose of Operation Urgent Fury was to prevent a takeover of this island by the Cuban-backed Grenadian People's Revolutionary Armed Forces. Casualties in this brief operation included 19 killed and 152 wounded.

"Operation El Dorado Canyon" was an anti-terrorism strike on Libya in retaliation for terrorist acts aimed at Americans. The 19-minute air-raid over Tripoli hit seven different targets a total of 227 times, destroying much of the Libyan infrastructure and temporarily intimidating Libyan dictator Colonel Muammar Quaddafi.

In 1987, it was necessary to send troops to the Persian Gulf to ensure access to the commercial sea lanes. Some of the military's special forces were used in this operation, notably the Navy Seals.

"Operation Just Cause" was launched in Panama in December 1989 to deter attacks on American citizens and to bring General Manuel Noriega to trial for his illegal drug dealings. With 27,000 U.S. troops deployed there, 23 were killed in action and 330 were wounded. Noriega was then deposed and brought to America to stand trial, and a democratic government was restored in Panama.

Carried out in every corner of the globe over three decades, America's mettle has been constantly tested, countering the new challenges to freedom during this era of "violent peace." Although the battles of the Cold War were for the most part limited, the threats were always real. On every front, soldiers waited and watched patiently, keeping the vigil of freedom.

In the midst of all of the turmoil, Americans witnessed some of their finest hours as they fought to carry the "beacon of freedom" around the world. And, during it all, the VFW has been constantly at the side of these Cold War veterans, offering them much-needed support and fighting continually for recognition of their sacrifices.

These brave men and women were separated from families and loved ones for long periods of time, just as if they had been involved in the fighting of a protracted war. And, even when they weren't actually firing or dodging gunfire, dangers lurked around every corner. Preparedness had to be constantly maintained, so that the soldiers might be ready for any attack that could signal trouble—or the escalation of a minor incident into a full-fledged war.

Waiting is often the hardest part of a mission, and the attendant uncertainties can wear down the nerves and patience of even the most experienced soldier. In addition, in many of these operations, soldiers had to endure the extremely inhospitable terrains and inclement climates of the remote countries where they were sent to serve.

When the Berlin Wall crumbled in November 1989, each and every one of these Cold War veterans could take a special pride in a job completed. Forty-five years is a long time, even for a war that is primarily of nerves and military diplomacy. An entire generation of Americans sacrificed, served, fought, watched, and waited to make sure freedom's flame continued to shine brightly.

The world owes much to these valiant warriors. We must remember and honor their brave deeds and make sure that they receive the proper credit, medical care, and support they may need in the years to come.

VFW cares particularly for these special veterans who fought to win the Cold War over communism and defended freedom around the world in other conflicts. We always stand ready to provide the assistance they may need. Let us never forget these proud victors of the intermittent, 45-year Cold War.

IX

OPERATION DESERT SHIELD / STORM

In the predawn hours of August 2, 1990, Iraqi troops stormed across the border and crushed neighboring Kuwait, touching off reverberations heard round the world. The United States quickly responded by drawing "A line in the sand," and Operation Desert Shield began.

Over 210,000 GIs were dispatched to a most inhospitable land to face one of the world's most unpredictable enemies. Operation Desert Shield tested America's mettle. It was the largest deployment of troops and buildup and training of military equipment in such a short time period in U.S. military history. Desert Shield put the military's logistical capabilities to the test. But America's service men and women were ready, and the long years of the Cold War military buildup and training paid off. Our military successfully countered yet another threat to freedom in the world.

In addition to the thousands of regular troops sent to the sands of Saudi Arabia to square off with Saddam Hussein's legions, this military operation resulted in the call-up of one of the largest number of reserve personnel in our history. Reserves, both men and women, had only hours to get ready to ship out. For the first time, many military women with children were called. Arrangements had to be made hurriedly for child care. In some cases, both husband and wife were sent for duty, often compounding the problem of getting one's business in order before leaving home.

Both American troops in the desert and those they left behind at home needed support to get through each day. The VFW rallied to meet their needs in a variety of ways.

Life in the Desert

The hustle and bustle of shipping out leaves little time on one's hands to think about what lies ahead. But once deployed with positions in place and the anxiety of the first encounter running high, then one must endure the wait. Boredom sets in.

As in so many wars and conflicts in the past, the geographical terrain brought its own challenges to the GIs and their equipment.

"I really can't describe how desolate it is. No trees. No rocks. No bushes. No life of any kind. The 'sand' really is more like a fine cement-mix powder, almost white," wrote Air Force 1st Lt. John Marks. But he went on to add that he was much better off than many of the others such as the "grunts" who were living in tents on the desert sands, enduring temperatures often hovering at 110 degrees. At least he had "decent quarters with lights, and air conditioning."

Furnace-like winds, poisonous snakes, sand storms rising out of the desert without warning, dehydration, and, of course, boredom were constant enemies. Some 10 species of poisonous snakes including the saw-scaled viper and Egyptian cobra, inhabit the Arabian Peninsula. Bites from a few of these reptiles can bring death in 10 to 15 minutes. The weather posed a continual threat. Sand storms pick up the sand, turn the sky yellow, and "wreak havoc on an occupied position." One defense analyst explained that the sand and dust storms were a "real test of human endurance and of performance for all that very sophisticated equipment."

Conditions in the field were spartan with 10 to 12 men in each patrol keeping watch on the sand dunes while lugging 85 pounds each of gear and clothing. Each load contained three canteens of water. Each person needed to consume up to six gallons of water a day to prevent dehydration.

Because of the threat of chemical warfare by Iraq, American military personnel had to wear special chemical warfare suits for long periods of time. The added weight and heat restricted movement and made the troops' burden even harder to bear.

VFW answered the call for support for our Desert Shield/Storm troops by being the first veterans group to visit the Saudi Front. VFW 1990-1991 Commander-in-Chief Jim Kimery accepted Prince Sultan bin Abdul Aziz's invitation for VFW leaders to visit Saudi Arabia. Senior Vice Commander-in-Chief Bob Wallace, Junior Vice Commander-in-Chief Jack Carney, Adjutant General Howard E. Vander Clute, Jr. and Washington Office Executive Director Larry Rivers made up the four-man fact-finding team dispatched to the Mideast to gauge the morale of the troops and to firm up a distribution network for VFW's Operation Hometown.

In a visit with General H. Norman Schwarzkopf, the commander-in-chief of the United States Central Command (CENCOM) headquartered in Riyadh, Saudi Arabia, the General expressed his desire to VFW leaders that the troops should have their own medal. And he said that he wanted that medal to be "the color of this sand."

On a tour of the Riyadh Air Base, one of the Wing commanders perhaps spoke for all when he expressed appreciation to the VFW leaders: "Tell your members that letters from home mean more than anyone can imagine."

Operation Hometown

"Most of our members remember when they served their country, thousands of miles from home, missing loved ones and friends," said Past VFW Commander-in-Chief Kimery. "Often these times were more bearable because of cards, letters and small personal gifts from the states." These memories of wartime comforts led to VFW's Operation Hometown, a ground-swell of support for the troops and those they left behind.

Over 100,000 packages were sent to the troops in the desert. Companies donated all kinds of personal products to make it just a little easier to bear the desert conditions and to let the troops know that the homefolk cared. Sunglasses, lip balm, baby powder, greeting cards, note pads, audio tapes, music cassettes, shampoo, paperback books, disposable razors, bandannas, games, hard candy, cookies, mouthwash, and chewing gum were sent to the servicemen and women serving their country in the hostile desert terrain. Clearly, people at home didn't forget the troops this time. Support from all levels was there with VFW leading the way, determined to ensure from the very beginning that Operation Desert Storm/Shield would not be another Vietnam.

The VFW-led effort didn't stop with supporting the troops in the desert. The loved ones left behind also received assistance through VFW's Operation Homefront. Many of the men and women who were called up in the Reserves or whose units were suddenly shipped out had only a moment's notice to get ready to leave. This placed particular hardships on families with children.

No one understands these difficulties better than VFW members. Most of them have personally experienced the pain that accompanies a sudden deployment. No matter how hard one tries to prepare himself or herself and families, separation still takes its toll.

VFW and its Ladies Auxiliary immediately went to work to help the families. Each Post had programs in operation practically overnight to offer much-needed support. Hotlines were set up to calm children's fears.

Volunteer tutors helped children with homework. Other volunteers gave hours of time as babysitters to relieve the one parent left behind trying to cope. Still others assisted with minor family emergencies and saw that families had plenty to eat when paychecks didn't make it on time.

When Sara Jordan's car broke down in Jessup, Maryland, VFW members repaired it so she could get to work. And when burglars broke into the home of Elsa White in Des Moines, Iowa, VFW members repaired the broken window and provided the support to see her through yet one more crisis.

Always serving, VFW and its Ladies Auxiliary charted the path for others to follow, so that America's servicemen and women, and their loved ones left at home, were cared for.

From Silence to Storm

After six months of watching and waiting, Operation Desert Shield became Operation Desert Storm on January 17, 1991, when Saddam Hussein and his Iraqi troops ignored the deadline to withdraw from Kuwait. U. S. Air Force planes began bombing Iraq.

This war was a television war. Millions sat nightly in front of their television sets actually watching SCUD missiles being intercepted and shot down by U.S. Patriot missiles. Allowed to stay in Iraq, Cable News Network reporters made news as well as reported it when they interviewed Saddam Hussein and showed censored video clips of bombings and destruction in the city of Baghdad.

But on the front lines, the "television war" was as brutal and unglamorous as any other. President Bush kept his promise that this would not be a repeat of Vietnam. The 532,000 GIs were allowed to use the air power and other fire power that was needed to win an all-out victory. Air raids dropped 141,921 tons of bombs on key Iraqi targets.

The capital city of Kuwait was liberated as the 1st Marine Division took Kuwait International Airport, while the 2nd marine Division blocked the northern exit from the city.

Meanwhile, the 24th Infantry Division reached within 150 miles of Baghdad and blocked the enemy escape route. The 24th Division then turned toward Basara and engaged the Iraqi Republican Guard—the Iraqi dictator's finest troops. In the largest tank battle since World War II, the U.S. and its allies destroyed more than 200 enemy tanks.

The entire Iraqi army was routed. Some 63,000 prisoners were taken. President George Bush declared, "Kuwait is liberated, Iraq's army is defeated." With that, he announced the end of offensive combat operations.

After a 38-day air campaign and a lightening 100-hour ground war, victory was declared by the United States and its allies.

Sporadic fighting continued as Kuwait and southern Iraq were mopped up. Coalition forces brought Iraqi dictator Saddam Hussein to heel as they formed a defensive arc in southeastern Iraq. The U.S. Navy remained in force offshore in the Persian Gulf and the Red Sea. At the same time, the U.S. Air Force retained command of the skies, conducting air patrols over the area of operations.

The war was over. The swift defeat of Saddam Hussein's Iraqi troops, however, had its price: 145 Americans were killed as a result of hostile action; 357 were wounded. Another 218 service personnel were killed in accidents and other non-combat incidents.

Once again, American lives had been given on foreign soil in defense of freedom.

After months in the deserts of Saudi Arabia or offshore in the Persian Gulf, Mediterranean Sea, and Indian Ocean, the soldiers, sailors, Marines, airmen, and Coast Guardsmen of America's Armed Forces returned home to a grateful nation. They were greeted with yellow ribbons and parades. It was a far different cry from the jeers and "no soldiers allowed" many Vietnam veterans met on their return home. VFW's Operation Homecoming made sure that the troops received the hearty, patriotic welcome they deserved.

The pride felt by Americans for their troops in Operation Desert Shield/Desert Storm seemed to reach beyond the desert warriors and envelope all veterans, particularly those of the not so distant war in Vietnam. Many of these veterans were recognized and appreciated for the first time. Numbers of them had been shunned and reviled. It appeared that the country at last was beginning to heal itself from the wounds of Vietnam. Operation Desert Storm was also the first test of our all-volunteer army, and it worked. A quick profile of Desert Storm troops shows that they came from across the spectrum of our society. About 80,000 National Guardsmen and Reservists played an important part of this operation, comprising around 15% of the total force. Northwestern University military sociologist Charles Moskos points out that small-town Americans made up the largest percentage of the troops, as has been true throughout military history. Presently, about two-thirds of America's military personnel come from the South and the Midwest. The remaining one-third is split between the West and Northeast.

Six percent of the troops stationed in the Gulf were women. Many served close to the front, although they are barred by law from holding combat specialty jobs. Of these, six women were killed. Half of them were Reservists who were killed in a SCUD attack.

Twenty-two helicopter pilots of the 101st Airborne Division were women. Women held vital roles in communications, transportation, intelligence, and medicine.

Another difference in this war was the large number of service members who were married: over 60% of Desert Storm veterans. Also, some 16,300 single parents and 1,200 military couples with dependent children served in the Gulf.

The VFW welcomes yet another generation of veterans. These veterans, as all of those who have come before them, have unique experiences and their own particular needs. And, as it has done for veterans of every war since its founding, the VFW will be there to meet those needs.

Perhaps it can best be summed up in the words of the VFW Past Commander-in-Chief in 1991, James L. Kimery:

"There is an intangible bond between those who have experienced the sacrifices intrinsic in overseas service and especially the mind-scarring rigors of combat in some distant land.

"Regardless of the era, enemy, weaponry, terrain or political outcome of the war, the unifying experience of serving together for a common purpose—be it as basic as the survival of one's own unit or as noble as promoting universal ideals transcends all differences of historical fate."

The VFW is always there for the men and women returning from war. As with those who served in Vietnam, Korea, and the two World Wars, VFW offers Persian Gulf veterans a place to validate their experiences of war, and an opportunity to serve their country, community, and family through an organization that understands and cares.

X

SPEAKING OUT FOR DEMOCRACY

In war or in peace, the Veterans of Foreign Wars embraces one central ideal: The safeguarding of our nation as the land of the free and the home of the brave. To uphold this ideal, VFW works on many fronts, even when war with other nations seems a remote possibility.

Today, the United States is more secure than several years ago; however, the spectrum of conflicts and range of world "hot spots" present a challenge every year. VFW believes today's security may be threatened if national defense and foreign policy are not equal to world challenges.

That is why VFW is committed to working for a strong national defense and steadfast foreign policy through its National Security and Foreign Affairs Department.

Current security and foreign affairs goals include:

- Maintaining a strong national defense.
- Maintaining conventional forces equal to the range of threats.
- Encouraging the government to use its full resources to provide the fullest possible accounting of POWs and MIAs from the Vietnam and Korean Wars.
- Supporting arms reduction negotiations that will enhance U.S. national security and reduce the risk of nuclear conflict.
- Supporting friendly democratic Central American governments and legislation to nullify the 1977 Panama Canal Treaties.
- Supporting strategic defense research which offers the possibility of protecting the United States and its allies from ballistic missile attacks.
- Opposing cuts in the strength of the National Guard and Reserve Forces.

• Supporting political, economic, and military assistance to allies.

• Supporting measures to deter, guard against and combat terrorists.

By actively supporting these initiatives, VFW hopes to bolster American military preparedness while fostering peace throughout the world.

Standing Up for that Grand Old Flag

VFW's Americanism program is designed to stimulate interest in America—including its history, institutions of government and our national heritage—through a number of celebrations and activities.

One such celebration is Loyalty Day, celebrated annually in May. This special day allows citizens to reaffirm their allegiance to America through parades, speeches, and other special events. Celebrated since the early 1930s, Loyalty Day was originally founded as a rebuttal to the Communists' May Day parade.

To generate patriotism in future generations, VFW sponsors programs to instill democratic values in American high school students. America's democratic heritage has been paid for with the lives of more than one million citizens in 10 major wars and many other campaigns on foreign soil. To ensure that this massive sacrifice is not in vain, the VFW sponsors the Voice of Democracy program, which reinforces ideals cherished by Americans, both veterans and non-veterans.

Voice of Democracy is a national broadcast script-writing competition which invites high school students to examine the responsibilities and challenges of citizenship, freedom, and democracy. This program was launched in 1946 with the endorsement of the nation's school principals and the U.S. Office of Education.

Each May, Voice of Democracy information is mailed to over 20,000 schools. Students in grades 10 through 12 are eligible to participate in this program. Entrants record a three- to five-minute broadcast script on an assigned patriotic theme. For 1991-1992, the theme was "Meeting America's Challenge."

The contest is conducted in cooperation with the National Association of Broadcasters and its state affiliates, along with state superintendents and commissioners of education. More than 2,300 radio and TV stations support the program.

Recordings are judged and winners are selected on four levels of competition—school, Post, District and Department. State winners receive a five-day, all-expense paid trip to Washington, D.C. In addition, they receive the opportunity to compete for 22 national VFW scholarships totaling $76,500. Scholarships, savings bonds, and other prizes amounting to more than $1,700,000 annually are awarded on all other VFW levels.

But all participants and sponsors share one major reward: self-satisfaction. It's not so much the size of the prize or even the degree of recognition that counts. What matters is that both students and VFW members made a contribution to the preservation of the American way of life.

We Will Never Forget

The VFW also continues to address one of the most perplexing and politically sensitive problems of the last two decades -accounting for the 2,348 Americans still missing in Indochina. VFW's Resolution 401 "America's Prisoners of War and Missing in Action: A Non-Negotiable Matter of Honor," states in part "that maximum U.S. economic and diplomatic pressure be sustained, for as long as it takes, to the end that those nations and movements which are hindering the search for the MIAs desist from this cruel practice and assist in the search effort as called for not only in the Paris Accords of 1973, but also by our common humanity...."

To lead the nation in an effort to account for our MIAs, VFW has strongly supported:

• Recognition of the POW/MIA issue as a top national priority.

• Post-sponsored public awareness programs across the country; and

• The continued service of Gen. John J. Vessey, Jr. as special Presidential emissary to Vietnam.

The identified remains of only 317 GIs from Indochina have been returned in the past 19 years. This works out to less than 15% of the 2,404 Americans (including 42 civilians) unaccounted for at the end of the war in 1973. Remains have been returned only when Washington has made some sort of concession or when the Communists were starved for international publicity.

Hanoi's regime has a well-established record of duplicity in dealing with MIAs. After the French Indochina War (1945-1954), only 7% of the remains of 22,000 Frenchmen killed in Vietnam were ever returned.

America has one overriding concern in Vietnam: That the fullest possible accounting of Americans missing there be made.

The VFW believes that every form of economic and diplomatic pressure should be employed to achieve that objective.

VFW Commander-in-Chief Bob Wallace visited Vietnam in July 1991 and again in May 1992 to speak directly to the Vietnamese officials in Hanoi who have the answers about unaccounted for Americans of the Vietnam War. The original invitation to VFW to visit Vietnam was extended through Senator John Kerry (D-Massachusetts).

Commander-in-Chief Wallace delivered an unequiv-ocal message from America's veterans stating that resolving the fate of American POWs and MIAs is an issue that will never fade.

VFW believes that a public commission, independent of the government and comprised of well-respected Americans, should be created to investigate extensively and determine decisively the fate of Americans unaccounted for during the Vietnam War. Declassifying documents is a necessary step in this process. But the solution to this problem will ultimately have to be found in Vietnam, Laos, and Cambodia.

Honoring America's Valiant Women Veterans

Some 1.2 million women served in uniform and are counted among America's veterans. More than half of the female veterans served during wartime. Some suffer the same delayed stress symptoms as their male counterparts.

In just one example of what these women have done for their country, Janet Harris recounts her experience as an operating room nurse at Phu Bai near Hue in Vietnam:

"We worked unrelentingly for seven days during the Battle of Hamburger Hill. After awhile the multiple amputees and all the young men with their faces blown away were no longer people, just cases. I carried those images with me for a long time, alone."

After returning home, she went through a period of constant depression, job hopping, and dissatisfaction with her life. Twenty years after her Vietnam experience, Janet Harris finally joined a therapy group that treats women suffering from posttraumatic stress disorder.

Some members of the group exhibit marked anxiety and elements of panic disorder. Having been caregivers for so long, it is often hard for them to be on the receiving end. These "invisible veterans" must be recognized and have their needs met as well.

Women have been actively encouraged to join VFW for more than a decade. Female veterans hold and have held positions of leadership at the Department and Post levels. The VFW strongly supports legislation beneficial to women veterans and has issued two long-standing resolutions that support construction of memorials to recognize and honor their service to their country.

Resolution 301 supports the Vietnam Women's Memorial Project in placing a realistic representation of a Vietnam era service woman on the grounds of the Vietnam Veterans Memorial in Washington, D.C.

Resolution 302 advocates creating an appropriate national memorial and assisting the Women in Military Service for America Memorial Foundation in its efforts to that end. VFW members nationwide feel that paying appropriate tribute to our women veterans is a top priority.

The Veterans' Voice on Capitol Hill

VFW's National Legislative Service (NLS) represents veterans in Washington, D.C. by meeting with congressional representatives to explain legislation that VFW believes needs to be introduced or passed.

VFW's legislative efforts have helped create many of the entitlements and programs for America's veterans and their families. Past accomplishments include the establishment of the Veterans Administration; the passage of the original GI Bill of Rights, plus making sure that its provisions also applied to the veterans of Korea and Vietnam; maintaining the VA hospital system; avoiding severe budget cuts as a result of the "Gramm-Rudman-Hollings Deficit Reduction Act;" and the creation of the cabinet-level Department of Veterans Affairs.

Today, fewer veterans are serving as members of Congress. That makes it more essential than ever that VFW reach elected officials with its positions on various issues during the '90s. Current legislative and other goals include:

• Protecting the U.S. Flag, through constitutional amendment, from desecration.

• Adequate funding for the Department of Veterans Affairs and the VA health care system.

• Establishing separate appropriation subcommittees for the Department of Veterans Affairs in both houses of Congress.

• Gaining cost-of-living increases, commensurate with the Consumer Price Index, for all VA beneficiaries and military retirees.

• Liberalizing criteria for herbicide-related claims.

• Maintaining Department of Labor veterans programs.

• Providing at least one open national cemetery in each state.

• Guaranteeing veterans preference in public and private labor markets.

• Full funding for the Disabled Veterans Outreach Program (DVOP).

• Ensuring appropriate benefits for Persian Gulf War veterans.

These measures are the least we can do to support and thank the veterans who have risked their lives for their country.

The NVS: Helping Veterans Get What They Deserve

VFW's National Veterans Service (NVS) helps veterans and their dependents and survivors obtain benefits from the Department of Veterans Affairs and other federal and state agencies.

Assistance begins with thousands of Post service officers, who direct claimants to trained Department Service Officers (DSOs) in each of the 57 VA regional offices. This network is supported by assistant DSOs, claims and appeals consultants, field representatives, and other staff in the VFW Washington Office and National Headquarters in Kansas City, Missouri.

While it might not seem necessary to provide such extensive assistance, benefits for veterans are numerous and complex. Filing applications alone involves miles of red tape. VFW helps veterans negotiate the maze of bureaucracy to ensure that they receive their due. The most sought-after benefits are disability compensation, pensions, and dependent benefits. Other major benefits include medical care, job training, home loans, household allowances, adapted housing for disabled veterans, educational assistance, burial entitlements, special automobiles for disabled veterans, and employment assistance, which is becoming more important than ever with the down-sizing of the armed forces.

The NVS also helps veterans with discharge reviews, correction of military records, medical and legal consultation, and many other types of problems or claims requiring contact with a federal or state agency. Furthermore, veterans can turn to the newly created U.S. Court of Veterans Appeals to appeal a denied claim. A future concern of the NVS will be the rapidly developing needs of aging veterans and the increased demands they will place on the VA's limited resources.

NVS field representatives also serve as "watchdogs," surveying VA hospitals, outpatient clinics, regional offices, national cemeteries and Veterans Centers to ensure high-quality service for veterans.

All forms of veteran assistance through NVS are provided free of charge. The NVS is supported by membership dues, Buddy Poppy sales, and contributions from the Ladies Auxiliary and other sources.

Through all these programs, the Veterans for Foreign Wars carries out its commitment to serve the individual veteran at the local level as well as in the halls of Congress and in The White House. VFW serves as the veterans' voice on Capitol Hill, always representing their interests as they have done so well for over 90 years. It works tirelessly to make sure that those who have sacrificed so much for our country receive the respect, care, and benefits they deserve. And VFW will never stop working to ensure that the flame of freedom continues to burn brightly.

CONCLUSION

As you read in the preceding pages, the VFW is above all a veterans service organization committed to "honor the dead by helping the living." This is not just a slogan but the purpose on which the organization was founded, and one which we try to put into practice on a daily basis.

To remain vital, a national organization must meet its constituency's needs, and these needs must be seen as important in the eyes of *all* Americans. The VFW has fulfilled both of these criteria for nearly a century, and that is why today we are as strong as ever. As each group of new veterans fights the good fight and comes home, the VFW is there to give them the assistance they need.

The VFW also offers a common bond of brotherhood to each new generation of veterans. War veterans constitute a special fraternity, with special needs and desires formed by their unique experiences. The desire to share the memories of such lifeforming experiences can be very powerful. As the public fanfare subsides and most Americans forget about the war that happened "somewhere else," the need to talk about war experience often only becomes stronger.

Socializing with another veteran who truly under stands is reassuring, providing an emotional outlet for feelings that a veteran can share only with fellow veterans. A local VFW Post is the ideal place to meet like-minded veterans as well as to renew and sustain friendships.

Service to the individual veterans is the hallmark of the VFW. The VFW can be a one-stop source of information on all benefits and entitlements, ranging from home loan guarantees to education eligibility to employment rights for all veterans. And a national network of Department and Post service officers, full-time and volunteer, stand ready to help veterans file claims or steer them in the right direction when the need arises.

Community involvement at the local level provides opportunities to volunteer time to the VFW for worthy projects, such as campaigns to get out the vote or to preserve our natural resources. Participation in more traditional activities, such as patriotic observances on Memorial and Veterans Days, can also be valuable contributions.

VFW volunteers can also help with youth league sports and teach children about safety—whether it's safety from drugs or bicycle safety. And volunteers who visit veterans in hospitals, bringing them small gifts or personal articles, can make a big difference to the comfort of the recuperating veteran, thereby increasing his chances of a speedy recovery.

The VFW also assists veterans who have hit hard times, by helping them pay their utility bills or buy their groceries. This small effort can mean a warm house in the winter or a Thanksgiving dinner for a veteran's family, who would otherwise go cold or hungry.

On the national political scene, the VFW has the size, influence, and prestige to make things happen. Our ability to protect veterans' rights is proven. Through the VFW's Washington, D.C., office, we have racked up an impressive array of legislative achievements, dating as far back as World War I. Veterans of World War II, Korea, and Vietnam have received entitlements that have made a real difference in their lives because of the VFW's tireless lobbying for GI bills. Because of these benefits, veterans have been better educated and provided with the tools to make meaningful contributions to American society in peacetime as well.

In light of recent, unprecedented world events—the collapse of the Berlin Wall, the swift victory of Operation Desert Storm, the end of the Cold War, and the collapse of communism in the Soviet Union and Eastern Europe—it would seem reasonable to assume that the veterans who served, sacrificed, and even died in the defense of freedom would be more appreciated today than ever.

Sadly, that is not the case.

The federal government's Department of Veterans Affairs (VA) has become a shadow of its former self. The VA health care system is in jeopardy. Politicians in Washington, D.C., have allowed a great agency to fall victim to severe underfunding and have not addressed a decade's worth of chronic, debilitating agency problems.

This blatant neglect has meant that veterans could not put their trust in this agency that was created to serve them. It has also eroded the VA's capability to provide and deliver quality services or quality health care to deserving and needy veterans.

The VA is no longer the leader in research and treatment of the aging. Limited funding, lack of commitment, and the absence of comprehensive, effective planning have placed VA hospitals and their outdated equipment far behind the norm in meeting health care demands with state-of-the-art medical technology.

It couldn't happen at a worse time, when many of our veterans are aging and in need of more and better health care services. A 1990 Independent Budget Project (IBP) concluded that "the nation's sickest, neediest and oldest veterans are in jeopardy of losing access to quality health care and necessary VA programs and services. This erosion will become a national disgrace."

How can we turn our backs on the very men and women who fought and worked to keep our country free?

The answer, of course, is that we cannot. And that is why the VFW is committed to ensuring that the government preserve a viable system for veterans, allocate resources according to actual need, and move quickly to expand eligibility and access to quality health care.

New and unexpected challenges will continue to arise for the veteran population in America. These challenges must be met head-on.

Of course, battles on Capitol Hill for federal funding grow tougher every day, because of the fierce competition among diverse interest groups for a share of a rapidly diminishing pool of federal dollars.

The recent "peace dividend" initiative, offered in response to cuts in defense spending, should be strongly considered as a way to keep the promises made to the 27,000,000 living veterans when they stepped forward to fight. Despite budget crunches, we must make sure that veterans do not go from parades to poverty!

The POW/MIA issue must also remain a top priority with our government, until the truth is known and as many of these brave men who are still alive are reunited with their anxious families.

There is so much to be done, and the VFW can only do it with your help. As government funds dwindle and veterans' needs increase, support from organizations like VFW is more critical than ever to the deserving veteran.

Help us to help them! Help us keep our nation strong and free, by instilling in the next generation a love of freedom and the values of patriotic citizenship.

The call could not be clearer. Why not help us answer it? The time is now. If our veterans' needs are not met, and if today's young people are not taught to cherish the basic democratic principles on which this great nation was founded and has been sustained, who will want to step forward and be the next patriots to answer the call when our nation's peace and liberty are threatened?

Please do your part to secure America's future by returning the coupon at the end of this book with your generous donation today. Our veterans will thank you for it.